A BRIEF SKETCH

OF

TRAVANCORE
THE MODEL STATE OF INDIA

A BRIEF SKETCH
OF
TRAVANCORE
THE MODEL STATE OF INDIA

S. RAMANATH AIYER

GYAN

Published by

Gyan Publishing House
5, Ansari Road
Daryaganj, New Delhi-110002
Phone: 011-47034999, 9811692060
E-mail: books@gyanbooks.com

Distribution Network
gyanbooks.com
India, USA, Canada, UK, Australia, France

ISBN: 978-81-212-9679-3 (PB)
First Published, 1903

2nd Impression 2023

Printed at: Gyan Press, Delhi.

A BRIEF SKETCH OF TRAVANCORE
THE MODEL STATE OF INDIA
Author: S. RAMANATH AIYER

A BRIEF SKETCH

OF

TRAVANCORE

The Model State of India

THE COUNTRY, ITS PEOPLE AND ITS PROGRESS

Under the Maharajahs.

BY

S. RAMANATH AIYER

Author of "Jubilee Leaves &c." "Our King-Emperor Edward VII, a Biographical Sketch" "Vanchisa Vijayam" &c.

1903.

PREFACE.

The work now submitted to the public presents a vast variety of information that I have gathered during a long period of unremitting devotion to the study of the country, its people, its history and its Government. The following extract from the *Madras Mail* explains the scope and object of the book :—"The book begins by discussing the natural features and the topography of the State, and dwells on the special features of its fauna, and flora. Then the early races of Travancore are traced to the various stages of their advent, and next come chapters devoted to the Nayars, the Numbudris and the Dravida Brahmins, which three classes comprise the mass of the population in the State...The Malayalam language and literature are lightly touched on in a short chapter, which is followed by an account of the principal religious temples and worship in vogue in the State, special mention being made of the catholic spirit which dominates the Government of His Highness the Maharajah in all matters pertaining to religion. Under the Section "Progress" a historical retrospect is given of Travancore and its ruling House and a succinct account of the economic progress made by the State during the times of the earlier and the later Rajahs. The chapter on the "Political Relations" with the paramount power is a clear statement of the circumstances under which the ruling House of Travancore came into relationship with the British. An excellent account is given of the present system of Administration and of the reforms effected in several Departments of the State in recent years."

In November 1900, when Lord Curzon honored the country with the *first* Viceregal visit, I submitted to His Excellency several articles published by me from time to time under the title of "Travancore Topics" and in kind appreciation of my proposal to work them out into a book of this kind, Mr. W. R. Lawrence, Private Secretary to H. E. wrote :—"The Viceroy wishes you every success in the proposed work.' Encouraged thus, I have performed a task which, I know, requires far greater equipment and external aid than I can command. I have kept in view fu'ness, precision and conciseness so very essential to a work which is the first of its kind. Nevertheless a few inaccuracies have crept in. I am very thankful to one of my European well-wishers who, in virtue of his high official position and of his special study of the country, can with authority speak on the subject, for having pointed out them to me.

On page 25, I should have said that Anjengo was made subordinate to the British Resident in 1810 when the post of Commercial Resident was abolished. It is now a part of the Malabar District.

On the same page, the statement that Quilon was the seat of the St. Thomas Christians is not quite accurate. It was 1000 years ago the chief seat of only *one portion* of the St. Thomas Christians. There are few there now.

I am in error when, on page 138, I state that Mar Dionysius and Mar Thoma have between them the whole of the Travancore Churches, for the fact is that the Romo-Syrians and the Latin Catholics have nothing to do with these two Bishops. By my remark on the same page that the two great Protestant Societies, the C. M. S. and the London Mission Society, owe their existence to Col. Munro and Veda Manikam, I mean of course that these persons brought the Societies into Travancore.

I shall be obliged to readers of my book if they will kindly communicate to me any errors that may still have escaped notice or any additional information on the topics treated of in it.

I may add however that the most authentic materials at present available have, after considerable research and study, been obtained and utilised in the book. I have cited in the body of the book the authorities relied on by me. I regret I had not the advantage of reading the excellent Census Report of 1901, since my work has been finished and submitted to His Highness' Government early in January 1902. It is impossible to exaggerate the magnitude of the debt I owe to His Highness' Government for the substantial aid given me in the publication of the work. I should fail in duty and in justice to my feelings if I do not take this opportunity of expressing my acknowledgments to Dewan Bahadur Krishnaswamy Row, and the late Mr. Thanu Pillai for their kind permission to consult the Huzur Records and Library and for their uniform kindness and advice.

S. Ramanath Aiyar.

Errata.

Page.	*Line*	*For*	*Read.*
1	6	Phycical	Physical
3	19	gives	give
5	26	Suzerainity	Suzerainty
15	23	Tripunathura	Thrikunnapuzai
69	20	of of	of
72	28	he	the
73	1	Michievous.	mischievous
,,	9	carly	early
,,	11	acquintance	acquaintance
,,	15	enormons	enormous
,,	19	neverthless	nevertheless
73	9	Solemnalliance	Solemn alliance
76	5	covil	civil
78	1	Brahminis	Brahmins
,,	16	ef	of
,,	24	frem	from
79	7	hisory	history
,,	19	presidcd	presided.
,	20	thc	the
81	22	illustrins	illustrious
,,	23	to	or
82	25	unmistakebly	unmistakably
83	6	are	or
,,	20	steets	streets
84	5	Yonnger	Younger
,,	26	Brahmani	Brahmin
,,	,,	wcwan	woman
,,	27	puberity	puberty
85	1	aprodigious	a prodigious
,,	4	an not	not an
86	1	West	East
87	8	Barhmins	Brahmins
89	30	South to north	North to South
90	15	territtrial	terrestrial
,,	16	assidions	assiduous
91	6	marriable	marriageable
92	28	Brahmin	Brahmins
99	12	production	productions
101	5	Malalam	Malayalam
108	12	625	925
,,	18	connectiou	connection

11	22	inpossible	impossible
12	2	incidentallly	incidentally
15	17	whole	white.
16	27	be	the
,,	29	nnknown	unknown
18	25	numerons	numerous
,,	28	to to	to
19	16	Kshtriya	Kshatriya
22	28	Superintendcnce	Superintendence
23	1	fradulent	fraudulent
,,	13	offlce	office
25	17	brougnt	brought
36	7	offencc	offence
39	17	tc	to,
51	2	Natiou	Nation
54	1	administraion	administration
59	25	increaseed	increased
61	14	territorties	territories
66	4	princes	princesses
67	11	of of	of
,,	17	ancester	ancestor
77	29	beng	being
,	,,	unoccuped	unoccupied
79	29	failsure	failure
83	18	conplated	contemplated
91	28	re ently	recently
96	6	provision	Supervision
100	16	Muncipal	Municipal
,,	29	,,	,,
108	27	educationest	educationist
109	17	crudite	erudite
113	6	girls	Girls'
114	13	adminitration	administration
,	20	exlightened	enlightened
118	28	Ruler's	Rulers
121	6	fourth	forth
122	27	indometable	indomitable
126	6	lives	lines
129	8	araise	arise
130	2	instituticns	institutions
,	26	distant	distance

CONTENTS.

The country.

The people.

Religion and caste.

Progress.

H. H. SIR RAMA VARMA

Moolam Thirunal Maharajah of Travancore.

TRAVANCORE

THE MODEL STATE OF INDIA

THE COUNTRY, ITS PEOPLE AND ITS PROGRESS

Under the Maha Rajahs

The Country.

CHAPTER I.—PHYSICAL ASPECTS.

Travancore is a representative Native State in the extreme south of the vast empire of continental India.

Like India, it is a most lovely kingdom to which Nature has been boundlessly bountiful. The Western Ghats define and defend its eastern boundary, while the western side is washed by the Arabian Sea. Between the lofty range of mountains and the extensive seaboard, the country opens out a panorama of perpetual verdure and luxuriant vegetation, diversified by every variety of wood and dale, of mountain and river, of lake and forest and of extensive topes of cocoanut and areca palms or cultivated fields. It has, time and again, attracted the attention of travellers and great personages. Many a Governor of the Madras Presidency, under whose sympathetic eye the State has prospered, has extolled its picturesque scenery. Sir M. E. Grant Duff describes it as "one of the fairest and most interesting realms that Asia has to show." Lord Connemora calls it "a fairy land." The talented pen of Mr. J. D. Rees has covered with additional charm its enchanting forest glades and flora. No wonder, therefore, that an ardent admirer of nature as Lord Curzon left the " city of palaces " to pay his first viceregal visit to this interesting country and admire " its exuberant natural beauties, its old-world simplicity and its Arcadian charm ".

Like India, the country with the influence of its situation near the equator, of its vicinity to the Indian Ocean, of its elevations of every variety, of its extensive sea coasts, of the direction of its mountain barrier and other circumstances that determine its climatic conditions, furnishes an interesting field for the study of its meteorology.

Like India, the country is clothed in magnificent primeval forests under which, according to the official report, there is a larger percentage of the land of this State than any other European country or the United States. Countless species of noble trees, medicinal plants and economic products abound with infinite attraction to the botanist.

Like India, the country furnishes an infinite variety of game to the sportsman and the naturalist.

Like India, the country opens a wide field of interest and attractiveness to the geologist whom the Quilon and Varkalai Beds, the Alleppey Mud Bank and the contortions of strata and embedded fossil would enable to discern its architectural designs and details and to boldly venture into the dark backward abysm of time; similanly, the plumbago mines now laid bare and busily worked and the rich prospect of mining it has initiated, will help the sturdy minerlaogist onward to dig deep into the barriers of the unknown.

Like India, Nature has exercised a considerable influence on the national history and character. The mountains have, in early times, decreed in favour of the breaking-up of the country into numerous petty states. The sheaves of plenty that Nature has freely bestowed upon the people also arrested their development into a healthy and compact nationality. The multitudinous population and their stratification into numerous castes and communities, their social condition, their peculiar manners, their diverse religious creed, influenced by internal dissension and by intercourse with foreign nations, gives the ethnologist a wide field for study and reflection.

Like India, the country has, from the ancient times, been known to the external world. The extensive sea-board affording many a safe roadstead for ships to anchor off and the immense natural wealth of the country have induced foreign nations to colonise it for purposes of trade from pre-historic times.

Like India, from whose trade the brilliant medieval republic of Italy drew no small share of her wealth, it is recorded by the late lamented Sir. W. W. Huntor that the pepper trade of Malabar and Travancore dates from far beyond the age of Sinbad the Sailor, and reaches back to Roman times and that philology proves that the precious cargoes of Solomon's merchant ships came from the ancient western coast.

Mr. Wigram, a distinguished member of the Indian Civil Service, maintains, in his "Malabar Law andCustom" that, when commerce was almost in its infancy, a trade sprung up between the Mediterranean ports and the ports of the west coast. The foreign intercourse resulted in the attainment, by the country, of historical importance and, by the people, of a higher civilization.

In a word, like India, the country presents a rich variety of natural scenery; of climatic conditions; of social and racial peculiarities. The student of Nature, of society and of religion will have each a wide field for his favourite avocations, research and study.

NAME.—This interesting country was known under different names at different periods of its history. *Vanchidesam* or the land of treasure; *Dharma Bhumi* or the land of charity; *Vanavarnad*, abridged into *Venaud*, or the land of the celestials; *Tripapur* or the land of the bearers of the sacred feet; *Rama Rajyam* or the kingdom of Rama Raja and *Kerala* or the land of cocoanut palms, are some of the names. Its present denomination is *Travancore,* which is a form of the Sanskrit *Srivardhanapuri* or the land where the Goddess of prosperity resides.

SITUATION.—It is a tributary Native State situated in the southwest extremity of the Madras Presidency, between Latitudes 8° 4' and 10° 22' N. and between Longitudes 76° 12', and 77° 38' E.

BOUNDARIES.—It is bounded on the North by the Cochin State and the Coimbatore District; on the East by the Madura and Tinnevelly Districts; and on the South and West by the Arabian Sea.

AREA AND POPULATION.—The extreme length from North to South is 172 miles and its extreme breadth is 75 miles, the total area is 6,370 Sq. miles. The population of Travancore according to the recent Census is 29,52,157.

RELATION WITH FOREIGN POWER.—The State is in subsidiary alliance with the British Government to which it pays an annual tribute of 8 lakhs of Rupees. Mr. Tupper calls the Ruler a "Feudatory". According to Mr. Lee-Warner, he is a "Protected Prince" in subordinate alliance with Government. To "subordinate" Col. Mallison prefers "subsidiary". Officially, however, the State is "an ally under the suzerainity of His Majesty". This was settled by the Treaty of 1805 which has placed on a permanent basis of security, for all time to come, the treaty of perpetual friendship and alliance between the Honourable East India Company Bahadur and the Maharaja Bahadur, concluded in 1795.

MOUNTAINS.—The country is bounded and buttressed on the east by a chain of mountains 200 miles long, generally spoken of as an uninterrupted continuation of the Western Ghats. These are, however, separated by the Palghat Valley which has proved a most useful feature in the Railway communication between the east and the west coast. The course of the mountains is very irregular. It breaks into hills of various heights. At several points, they rise to an elevation of over 8000 feet above the sea. They slope in successive tiers towards the tableland, until it gently falls to the level of the sea. The average altitude of these summits is 4,000 feet. The mountain chain bears different names in different parts. The Northern portion is known as the High Range or the *Anamalay*. Its Sanskrit name is *Gajasailam* or the Elephant Hill. It has a remarkable rock, two miles long and one-fourth of a mile in breadth. This is supposed to represent the elephant sent by a king of the Chola country to devastate and destroy the beautiful city of Madura. There is a ruined temple hewn out of a side of the rock said to have been destroyed by Tippu Sultan. The chief summit of the Anamalay Range is called *Anamudi*. It is 8000 feet high, and has a climate similar to Ootacamund. The plateau is often visited by ibex hunters. They obtain honey by swinging themselves over the precipice with long chains of ropes or rattans and sell the article to the people of the plains. Further south, are the Cardamom Hills and the Peermed plateau. In the former, cardamom which was till quite recently a State-monopoly, grows abundantly, and the latter is called after the Mahomedan Saint, Peer Mohamed, who is said to have resided there. It is the seat and centre of planting industries. It is largely resorted to by the Europeans who have largely taken up for the purpose, Camp Gorge, Ponmudi, Ashambu and other portions of the range. Beyond these, the range descends to the Shencotta pass. Here it is only 800 feet high, but rises to 4000 feet further south and stretches for over 60 miles. Its termination is Agastiakudom or the abode of Agastia, one of the seven sages who, having escaped at the flood of Manu, is supposed to have dwelt apart in proud isolation on the top of this peak where popular tradition considers him to reside even to this day. Its height is 9150 feet and on this was built, in 1854, an Observatory under the direction of Mr. Broun who recorded meteorological observations for a long time. The southern most peak of the Travancore Ghats is Mahendragiri. This is the "*Malli quorum mons mullus*" of Pliny. This is the hill from the summit of which Hanuman, the Monkey chief and confederate of the classic Rama, is said to have jumped to the beautiful Lanka, the modern Ceylon or the Golden isle. In the entire range, the other peaks of note are Amarthamala, Kodayathur Mala, Nedumpara Mala, Papanasa Mala, Marithva Mala and the Peria Mala.

RIVERS.—Owing to its mountainous character, the country, like few provinces of similar extent, is washed by very many large and fine rivers. They rise in the mountain slopes, take more or less a westerly or southerly direction and discharge themselves into the sea either directly or through the lagoons. The bed of the rivers is frequently rocky at the elevated parts but in most instances sandy, as they approach the plains. The banks are, near the Ghats, precipitous, but get lower and lower as they quit the elevated parts. They are successively over-hung by verdant forests, groves of luxuriant vegetation or cultivated fields. The course of the rivers is winding, especially towards the coast and the depth is, on the average, from 12 ft. to 15 ft., while the tides, whose vicissitudes are felt but slightly, rise about 3 ft. and are subject to diversity. With the beginning of the monsoon, the rivers rapidly swell and spread without control, rolling a full and copious tide, but they diminish with equal rapidity while the violence of the monsoon draws to a close. By far, the largest is the Periyar, as its name signifies. It is unsurpassed in size, beauty and usefulness by any of the streams of the west coast. Messrs. Ward and Connor, in their geographical memoir of the State, describe the river thus:—"This noble river has its source in the Alpine chain of the Peninsula, separating Tinnevelly from this State, and mingles its waters with the ocean at Pallipuram, near Kodangallur. It forms many cascades in its earlier course. Innumerable streams swell its waters by the tribute of their copious tides. The whole of those streams pass through the wildest country possible, dashing over their stony channels confined to a contracted breadth by the mountains on their borders or hurled in a succession of cascades; nor does the advance of the parent stream proceed with less embarassment, though its course is marked with more variety; at intervals, hurrying with resistless violence over the asperities of its rugged and narrow bottom and dilating into placid ponds whose glassy surface reflects the dusky declivities that overhang its rocky margin, or precipitated in cataracts as its impetuous tide dashes tumultuously over the rocks that intersect its progress, or struggling through the contracted channel to which they confine it. Such is the general character of the river before reaching Neriamangalam where, escaping from the winding depths through which it had been forcing a passage, it flows in a comparatively placid stream towards its embrochure. With the exception of the last 35 miles of its total length of 142 miles, this fine stream passes through a complete wild."

A

Its enormous volume of water is now diverted into Madura by the Periyar water-works for which the Durbar has leased out to the British Government over 8,000 acres of land above the river-line for a consideration of 40,000 Rupees. It is worthy of note that Mr. Nelson records, in his "Madura Manual", that this project was under contemplation "even during the days of the Madura Naicks".

Proceeding South, the next is the Muvattupuzhai river. It is swelled by the waters of several tributary streams of which the largest flows into it near the place that gives the river its name. Then comes the Meenachil river which, formed by the confluence at Errattupettah of several streams that descend from Kodayattur and Kodamurutti hills, pours its waters into the Vembanad lake which is the reservoir of the copious tribute of many large rivers. Then comes the Pamba or Ranni river which is one of the finest streams of Travancore. It owes much of its waters to the confluence of the three large streams.—Kallar, Kakkattar, and Pamba, which have their sources in the hilly tract above the Ranni. About 20 miles above the mouth it unites with the Achenkoil or Kulakada river which issues from the foot of the pass of the same name. Five miles down, this rapid stream is joined by the Manimala river which proceeds from the Peermade plateau. Its waters are much used for cultivation. Further south is the Kallada, the third largest river in the country. It is swelled by the tribute of several large streams that flow from the higher ghauts in a succession of cataracts. The largest and most remarkable of them is known as *Meenmutti*. It flows into the Ashtamudi lake by several mouths which, in some parts, are 300 yards wide. The Ittikarai is a less important stream which flows into the Parur Lake, while further south we have the Attangal river called also Bhavanipuram. We have again the Karamanai river and the Neyyar, both of which have their sources at the Agastya slopes, and discharge themselves into the sea—the one near Poonthura and the other near Poovar. The former has a bridge remarkable for its strength. It was opened on 17th December 1853. Its architecture is so perfect that it has never required any beyond slight repairs. The river that next claims attention is the Thamravarni which descends from the mountains north of the Mahendragiri peak. Several dams divide and divert its waters for irrigation purposes. To it, Nanjanaud which is justly known as the granary of the South, owes much of its fertility. It forms several water-falls during its course. One of these falls is near Triparap, renowned for an old Siva shrine. It receives the Kothai that comes down from the Mulanchi mountains. Project works are now going on to divert its waters for irrigation purposes. The execution of the project is calculated to confer fertility on a large tract of the south country. The Paralayar is the most southern of the rivers which though the last is not the least in value, as that is the only river whose waters are wholly absorbed in irrigating a vast extent of land.

Lakes—The lakes may next be viewed. It will be seen that a succession of lagoons or backwaters extends along the coast and forms an important means of water communication. As observed by Lieutenants Ward and Connor, "they enrich the neighbourhood, unite the distant parts and increase the value of natural productions by the facility they give to carriage. The whole traffic of the western part of the country is done by them." The large lakes are fed by the copious waters of innumerable rivers. The smaller ones are merely the expansion of the beds of rivers as they approach their mouth. The most important of the lakes have outlets into the sea. These outlets are often closed by bars of sand. When the monsoon sets in, the water jumps impatiently from the beds of the lakes and either breaks through or flows over the bars, according to the fury with which the periodical rains burst. It is then terrible to think of being caught in the grip of the enraged elements on the troubled waters, but it is a source of infinite consolation and comfort to contemplate the weird view of the lakes, when they resume calmness and the setting sun shines on the unlimited expanse of water through the beautiful groves of the cocoanut palms which skirt their margins or the smiling moon spreads her silver lustre amidst the solemn stillness of the night. The splendour is enhanced when beautiful boats provided with numerous paddles, press their progress with singular rapidity. The lakes then present the appearance of a perpetual garden of lasting delight. The Vembanad is the largest lake in Travancore, being 32 miles long. Its extreme breadth is 9 miles. Its waters are swelled by the copious tribute of several large rivers of which the Pamba, the Manimala, the Meenachil and the Muvattupuzha are the principal ones. This lake passes along 5 to 7 taluks of the country. In some parts, the soundings show considerable depth; in other parts, the lake is very shallow. It has a small island in the centre, known as the Patiramanal or the mysterious mound of midnight. It is filled with cocoanut plantations or luxuriant vegetation, and presents an infinitely charming appearance. It was, according to tradition, called into existence by the piety of a Namburi Brahmin who, while travelling in a country canoe jumped out there into the lake to perform his religious rites at the appointed hour. The Kayankulam lake is 19 miles long and has wide expansions at both the extremities, into which the Cochin Canal from the north and the Quilon Canal from the south open. It has an outlet bar of the same name which admits small coasters from the Arabian sea. This made Kayankulam a place of considerable commercial importance during the days of Dutch influence before the subversion of the independent state of Quilon. The Ashtamudi or the lake of 8 creeks lies near historic Quilon and is swelled by the tribute of the Kallada river. It has also an out-let into the sea through the Nadayara Bar. Among small lakes may be mentioned the Parur lake which is a dangerous portion of the water communication owing to the strong action of the under-current work at the bar, when it is broken through during the violence of the periodical rains; as also the Anjengo lake which takes its name from the town of which it lies along-side.

CANALS.—The water-ways of Travancore, says Mr. Nicholson are specially from the centre to the North, highly ramified and already excellent for all classes of country traffic. They might on main lines be developed into trade routes. The cost of travel and transport on Travancore waters, he adds, is perhaps ¼ of ordinary cart charges, while transit is quite as speedy and far less risky for goods and far more comfortable for passengers. He thinks that for most of the water-ways, little or no maintenance is required for ordinary traffic, especially in the Northern Division where, as in Shertalai, the country has vast areas of backwater or where, as in Changanacherry over large reclaimed areas, there can be no roads but only rivers and canals, so that travellers, even children, paddle rather than walk. One stretch of water extends along the entire length of the country from Trivandrum northwards.

It was during the benevolent reign of Her Highness Parvathi Rani, that most of the links of this uninterrupted line of communication were executed. The canal between the Trivandrum Landing place and Chanankarai, commenced in 1823, was brought to a completion in 1826 at a cost of a lakh of Rs. The length of the canal is $11\frac{3}{4}$ miles exclusive of the lake it passes through. From Chanankarai to Kozhithottam there is a canal again. The Varkalai Barrier canal, cut open through two tunnels of about 1500 feet and 2500 feet each, was opened for traffic in 1877. There are a series of lakes from Nadayara to Paroor. The Paroor canal, connecting the Nadayara lake and the Parur lake, was completed in 1820 at a cost of Rs. 90,000. It is 6 miles long. The Quilon canal which links the Parur lake with the Ashtamudi lake was also opened about the same time. There is then the Chavarai canal between the Ashtamudi lake and the Ponmana waters. This is followed by the "Ayiram Thengu" back Water; then comes the Kayankulam lake. With it, the Tripunathura back-water joins the Thottapalli Cherai, whence the Pamba river flows into the Vembanad lake. There are several branch canals. The Alleppey canal communicating with the back-water is of commercial importance. It is a matter of interest to note that the great Anantha Victoria Marthanda Canal, projected and commenced in 1860 for connecting Trivandrum with Cape Comorin, has had to be abandoned, partly owing to the obstacles presented by the Covelam cliffs and the Midalam Barrier, and partly on account of the pressing tunnel work at Varkalai which drained off the work-men, the officers and the capital allotted to this scheme. The Department of Public Works maintains 152 miles of water-way and it has to be borne in mind that this is a trifle out of the actual water-ways.

ROADS—Of road communication there are three great trunks in the country. The great southern road runs from Trivandrum to Tinnevelly. It is perhaps the heaviest worked road out-side the Madras city and is, according to Mr. Nicholson, repaired like a high-way in England. It has several travellers' Bungalows interspersed at intervals of from 8 to 12 miles. The great Northern road runs parallel to the water communication through the centre of Travancore to the northern frontiers, providing easy access to fertile forest tracts for cultivation. The great eastern road runs towards the British Districts of Madura and Tinnevelly northwards, and towards Palamcottah eastwards. The sketch will be incomplete, if we do not refer to the High range road which has opened up communication between the Ghauts and the low country. It was for the benefit of the European planters. Carriages can now go almost to every part of their estates. A fresh impetus is thus given to develop the planting resources of the country. Besides these, there are several minor lines of roads. But it is of course impossible to enumerate all the roads, great and small, and it is more-over foreign to the scope of this paper. Suffice it to say that there are 2,000 miles of cart road and about 900 miles of village road maintained by Government and more than 300 miles of new roads have been traced.

ROAD-STEADS.—The Travancore coast is extensive. It begins at Cape Comorin and terminates about mid-way between Alleppy and Cochin. The coast is generally low and sandy, fringed with cocoanut palms. The sea-line is however interrupted by the precipitous rocks of Cape Comorin, the jutting promontories of Kadiapatanam, and Vilinjam, the rugged cliffs of Varkalai, the narrow reefs of Tangacherry and by the wide mouths of several rivers. The town of Alleppy is the principal sea-port of Travancore. It has the most remarkable haven of smooth-water available all the year round, called the "mud-bay" by the early navigators. It is a place of considerable foreign trade and Head-Quarters of the Commercial Agent to the Travancore Government. Bartalomeo has put on record that Alleppy was opened to foreign trade in 1762 and mentions the canal which runs parallel to the coast and back-water. It has a light-house 100 feet above the sea-level, visible from all directions sea-wards for 15 miles.

B.

The next important port is Quilon. It is a place of great commercial activity and of considerable historical importance. Close by on the margin of the sea, lies the small port and British possession of Tangacherry which has a flag-staff and a Master Attendant's house. Anjengo is another small port mid-way between Quilon and Trivandrum. It will be interesting to English readers to learn that it was the birth-place of the great historian Robert Ormes and the chief military depôt during the wars of the country. It passed under the sway of the British in 1795 and still continues to be in their possession. Trivandrum, the present capital of the state and the seat of the Residency, is the next place that affords a safe harbour. Further south is the small port of Colachel where the first British ship anchored off in 1871. The port has a flag-staff and a Master Attendant's house; and lastly there is Cape Comorin, the southern-most extremity. It has a natural harbour which is a safe road-stead for ships to approach with the least apprehension during the monsoons. Steps are being taken to develop it into a flourishing commercial port.

CHAPTER II.—TOPOGRAPHY.

We have viewed the country from within as well as from without. We have described its general characteristics, name and limits; have noticed its relation with foreign power; have dealt with its mountains and rivers; lakes and canals; roads and roadsteads. We shall now proceed to consider its territorial divisions and topography.

The whole area of the state is represented by the following 31 taluqs:—Thovalai, Agasthiswaram, Eraniel, Kulkulam, Vilavancode, Neyyattinkarai, Trivandrum, Neduvangaud, Chirayinkil, Kottarakarai; Pathanapuram; Shenkottah; Quilon; Kunnathur; Karunagapalli; Kartigapalli; Mavelikarai; Chengannur, Thiruvella; Ambalapuzhai; Shertalay; Vycome; Yettumanur: Kottayam; Changanacherry; Minachil; Muvattupuzhai; Todupuzhai; Kunnathnaud; Alengad and Parur. Of these, Thovalai and Agasthiswaram which form the regions of Nanjanad were formerly ruled by Korava chiefs. The taluqs of Eraniel, Kalkulam, Vilavancode, Neyyattinkarai, Trivandrum, and Chirayinkil comprised the old limits of Travancore. Neduvangaud and Kottarakarai, called Yellevarnad, was an independant principality ruled by chiefs whose race is now extinct. The districts of Quilon, Karunagapalli, Kartigapalli and Mavalikarai constituted the principality of Kayankulam, known as Oonad, while Ambalapuzhai and portions of Shertalay and Vycome, which went under the name of

Vembanaud, were ruled by the Chembakacherry Rajahs. The territory included by Muvattupuzhai and Ettumanur was held under sway by the Tekkumkur and Vadakumkur Rajahs. The Taluqs of Minachil and Alengad were under the authority of a Samunder chief. Kunnathnad was the possession of the Edapalli Raja and Parur had its own independant chief. These small states are now incorporated into the Travancore territory with the exception of the Attangal tract which is the hereditary possession of the Ranees of the Royal family; the Kilimanur estate which constitutes the property of Koil Tampurans who are allied to the Royal house; the Vanjipuzhai estate belonging to a priest of some spiritual dignity: the Edapalli estate held by another chief of still higher spiritual rank; and few other tracts belonging to Pagodas which are richly endowed. It may be noted however that the Criminal jurisdiction over these tracts vests in the Sircar.

The country is, for administrative purposes, split up into the following divisions:—The Southern division embracing the first five districts; Trivandrum division consisting of the next four; Quilon division having the next seven and Kottayam division comprehending the last eleven districts. The districts are known as Mandapathumvathukal, meaning the temple's front, because in 1750 after the conquest and consolidation of the whole kingdom, the then reigning sovereign dedicated the country to Sri Padmanabha; managed the administration in the name of god-head and denominated all public servants to be Sri Pandarakaryam chaivargal or those who carry out the divine function of administration. The sub-divisions of these districts are differently known in different places. In some districts (especially in the north) Proverti is the name. In others (mostly southern districts) they are called Kelvi. Maniyam is another name applied to them. It appears that tracts bearing the first name which means action, were acquired by conquest: that Maniyam lands were held by prerogative and that Kelvi areas were got by negotiations. Judging from the nature of the acquisitions of the several taluqs in which they are situated, this explanation seems to have the support of the facts of history.

We now pass on to notice the principal places of historical, archæological and other allied and varied interest. We attempt to notice them in their natural order as one travels northward from Aramboly, the southernmost gate of the country, leading to the fertile flats of Tinnevelly. It had a military line now almost in ruins, of about seventeen miles in length, guarding the Southern frontier. It is the seat of the customs house to collect tolls on dutiable goods. We then pass on to Alagiapandipuram, or the beautiful city of the Pandian chiefs, which was the capital of the Nanjakuravar chiefs who ruled Nanjanaud for a long time. Eight miles south is Boothapandy, an ancient town, also once in the possession of the Pandian Rajas. We then come to Nagercoil, once the seat of Government and now the seat and centre of the Christian Mission work, in south Travancore. We next reach Kottar—the Kottara of Pliny, mentioned by Ptolemy and also in the *Periplus*–the greatest commercial town in South Travancore. It has an ancient Pagoda with the inscriptions of Parakrama Pandian. It is also the seat of St Francis Xavier's Church. Near this is Vadiveeswaram, the chief habitat of the Brahmins in South Travancore. Proceeding South, we get to Suchindram, one of the largest places of Hindu worship in South Travancore. It has a celebrated shrine sacred to Siva where, according to tradition, Indra, the god of the celestials, was absolved from the depravity of sin. We touch Myladi, or the place where the peacock plays, near the foot of the Southern hills, the celebrated home-stead of the first Protestant missson-ary church in South Travancore. We gain Oodayagiri, or the hill of the dawn, which has a fort containing the tomb of captain D'Lanoy to whose military talents Travancore cannot be too thankful. Not far off is Padmanabhapuram the former seat of Government previous to its removal to Trivandrum. It has a celebrated Palace, Pagoda and fortifications with bastions. There is a subterranean passage from the palace leading from the fort outside to the paddy flats of Charode. This was frequently resorted to during the early wars of the country. In its vicinity is Keralapuram, or the city built by Kerala Varma, one of the early sovereigns of the country. It has considerable historic associations. Close to it is Thiruvancode which gives the country its name. It was the former residence of the Maha Rajahs. Adjoining it is Erȁniel which was also once the residence of the Travancore Royal Family whence one of the kings suddenly disappeared, while sleeping in the palace. It is suggested that Eraniel is derived from *Era* which, in Tamil, means king and, *niel* or disappearance, and the town therefore takes its name after the mysterious disappearance of the king. But as it appears to have existed and borne this name long before this incident, we think it is called so on account of the saltish nature of its soil, in that, *Era* in sanscrit signifies salt soil. Turning eastwards, we come upon Thiruvattar where the river Tamravarni winds round the ancient pagoda of which the design is after that of the chief State Pagoda in the capital. Travelling south, the only place of historical association is Balaramapuram in Neyyattinkarai, founded by Dewan Oomuithambi about 1808, and named after the then reigning sovereign. We are now at Trivandrum, or the city of the eternal one, the present capital of the state and the residence of the Maharajah. It has a temple of antique celebrity resorted to by a large concourse of pilgrims from the snowy heights of the

Himalayas to the sunny vales of Cape Comorin. It has very many fine public buildings constructed more than half a century ago, where the principal offices of the state are accommodated. The most interesting edifice is the Musuem which was thrown open to the Public in 1857. Four miles south is Tiruvallam, or the land of the Holy Lord, which has a Pagoda, the only pagoda sacred to Brahma. It is considered as sacred as Gaya in Northern India, and Sradhas and other ablutions to the manes are therefore performed here. Tradition says that Vishnu reclaims his head in this locality. We next discover ourselves at Thrippapur or the village of the sacred feet of God. This is the village from which the members of the Royal family of Travancore derive their titular name of Thrippapoor Swarupam. We have already referred to Neduvangaud or the country of the big forests, which was once ruled by a race of chiefs now totally extinct. Travelling northwards, we make towards Attangal, the hereditary domain of the Ranees of the Royal house. To this place H. H. the Maharaja repairs at least once every year to worship the family Deity. In its vicinty is Kilimanoor or the city of parrots and deer, which is the home and property of Koil Tampurans or local dukes who are allied to the Royal house by marriage and adoption. Travelling north, we pass the British possession of Anjengo, the birth-place of the great historian, Robert Ormes.

Here the first English factory was established in 1673. It marks the commencement, even so early, of the political relation between Travancore and the East India Company. The jurisdiction over the place which vested in the Commercial Resident appointed first in 1777, is now in the hands of the Political Resident in Travancore and Cochin. The place, abounding as it does with the tombs and memorials of several British officers and their families, cannot fail to be of considerable interest to English tourists. The next place of importance we reach is Varkalai. It is of much geological interest. It has two water-tunnels which connect together and throw open an uninterrupted course of water-communication from Trivandrum to the North. It has also an antique shrine of great sanctity. We next arrive at Quilon, the Coilam of Marcopolo ; the greatest port of Malabar in early times; the chief seat of the St. Thomas Christians; the Head-Quarters of the Dewan and the Resident till 1829 and now the cantonment of the British subsidiary force. Reference has already been made to its independent existence prior to 1745, under the rule of the Rajas of Kottarakarai and Panthalam. To Dalava Rama Iyer is due the credit of having subdued and annexed it to Travancore. Kayankulam, the capital of the Quilon principality before its conquest, is the next place that claims our attention. It communicates by back-water with Cochin in the north and Quilon in the south and by road with Madura and Tinnevelly on the other side of the Ghauts. It was therefore a centre of trade during the early days of the Dutch influence. A Syrian Christian Church appears to have been founded here so early as 829 A. D. The historically-inclined traveller may next set his foot on the soil of Ambalapuzhai or the city of the celestial Ganges, which lies under water for part of the year. This was till 1754 the Head-Quarters of the Chempakacherry Rajahs who ruled part of the country. Alleppy which has been already referred to as the chief port of Travancore is the seat of the Commercial Agent of the Travancore Government. It is well worth remembering that Bartalameo records that this port was opened to foreign trade in 1762 and mentions the canal which runs parallel to the coast and back-water. We next find ourselves in Kottayam, the chief home of the Syrian Christians and the Head-Quarters formerly of its independent native chiefs and now of the Church Mission Society since 1816. We now reach the northern frontiers of Travancore and the last place we shall make a halt at, is Edapalli or the village of detached margin, which was the capital of the principality of the same name. Here lives the Numburi Brahmin of rank who is the family priest of the Royal house of Travancore.

It will be seen from the above what a wide

field the country presents for making antiquarian and archæological researches. The establishment of an archæological Department in 1071 "with a view to the collection and investigation of the available data relating to the political and economical history and ethnology of the country" is a conspicuous proof of the interest that His Highness the Maharajah takes in such fields of knowledge. It is gratifying to find that the untiring researches of the late Professor Sundram Pillay have brought to light for the *first* time some 30 sovereigns who had reigned over this ancient land of Venad. While in British India the fast dying inscriptions declare "*observe now or never*" and the declarations are heeded with uncommon zeal and interest, and organisations started to decipher those inscriptions and furnish materials for what is known as the unwritten portion of history, and while such organisations are maintained *even* in countries where the results got at by investigation are yet *disappointing*, too much stress cannot be laid on the necessity for the enlargement and encouragement of an establishment which has yielded and would, under proper supervision, yet yield good and substantial results.

CHAPTER III.—METEOROLOGY.

We have sketched the physical aspects of the country in our survey of it from within as well as from without. It is now proposed to deal with topics of scientific interest relating to the country, such as its climatic conditions or meteorology; its material frame-work or geology; its vegetable products or flora; its animal wealth or fauna, and the like. We know each of these subjects, if adequately treated, would cover many volumes, and such an adequate treatment requires the help of a large body of specialists—a help which, however, we cannot lay claim to. Nevertheless, it goes without saying that some account of them may be neither uninteresting nor unuseful to the general reader. We offer the following notes, therefore, not for the instruction of the specialists, but to the general reader who wishes to study the country in all its aspects. We may add, however, that these notes are based on official reports and other reliable documents, and are therefore far from inaccurate or unacceptable. These will suffice to introduce the subjects until they are fully and finally investigated.

GENERAL.—Mr. V. Nagamiah says, in his last Census report, that the meteorological effects of the whole of india, if not of the whole world, are in a small compass presented to us in Travancore; that on some of the peaks we have the pinching cold of the northern regions of Europe; that lower down, on an elevation of between 2000 and 3000 feet one meets with the bracing temperature of England; that an Italian sun, with its clear and cloudless sky and a genial warmth, is experienced all over the country for a few weeks after the cessation of the heavy monsoons and that from January to May which constitute the months of the hot season, there is an intense and oppressive heat which at times becomes so intolerable that some of the taluqs then present the aspect of a true equatorial region from which it is not far distant.

Causes.—Among the chief of the different causes to which the peculiar characteristics of Travancore are ascribed, may be mentioned the following—(1) Its situation near the equator which makes it hotter than the countries interior. (2) Its vicinity to the Indian Ocean which prevents the air from becoming either too warm or too cold. (3) The influence of the mountain ranges which shut off the country from the rest of India.

It has been observed before that the mountains generally sink down from the western border till they fall to the level of the low country. In effect, the plentiful rainfall brought by the south-west monsoon is caught and deposited on the Travancore side only. This begins about the middle of Edavam and ends in Kanny. The showers are heavy and frequent thunder and lightning prevail.

The quantity of rain is less in the southern part of the country and increases along the sea-line to the north. The north-eastern parts are supplied with rain by the effects of the monsoon of that direction. It commences in the month of Thulam. The amount of rainfall is calculated for a number of years. It was in 1836 an observatory was established at Trivandrum. It is situated on a hill about 200 ft. above the level of the sea. The first meteorological observations were made by John Caldecott, the first astronomer. General Cullen, the British Resident had also caused observations to be taken, ascertaining the rainfall from 1852-56 at Cochin, Quilon, Alleppy, Cape Como in and other places. In 1852 Mr. John Broun became the Government astronomer. It was during his time the most extensive observations were recorded. The Branch Observatory established by him on the Agasthya Peak, however, fell to pieces during his absence and was finally abolished.

The average amount of rainfall varies in different places. Judging by the quantity of rain gauged in the several stations from 1882-91, it is observed that nearest the Cape it is only 58 inches, at Trivandrum it is 73, at Quilon even more—94 inches; that the highest fall is in Peermaad where in 1057 it was so great as 297 inches and that during the same year the fall at Alleppy was 160 inches, Quilon 101 inches, Trivandrum 81 inches and Padmanabapuram, 85 inches. Owing to this perennial moisture, Mr. Bourdillon thinks that probably nowhere in the world are the conditions of growth so favourable as in Travancore and consequently we find the ground completely covered with trees or shrubs wherever it is not cleared for cultivation.

WINDS.—The country has a constant flow of breeze. From Kumbham to Kanni it blows from the west or north-west; during other months it takes a more northerly direction. The Kumbham-Kanni winds are laden with moisture and dissolve into rain, in a mountainous country like Travancore. Mr. Bourdillon notes a peculiar case of saturation of air with moisture during the continuance of the rains. He says "at Alleppy I have frequently noticed a difference of only half a degree between the wet and dry bulb Thermometers." The direction of the sea-breeze is said to be from north to west and ultimately to south-west, while that of the land winds is from north-east and east. The sea-breeze sets in violently at times and lasts through the year. The land wind blows after sun-set and continues till next day noon. It blows rather violently at the entrance of the mountain passes. Every traveller knows that through the Aramboly pass it rushes forth vehemently and upsets many a cart and traffic and even men.

TEMPERATURE.—The temperature of the country is more or less uniform. Its proximity to the sea does not allow it to vary as it would in the interior regions. The temperature, however varies in proportion to the height of different places above the level of the sea. In the plains it is said to range between 65° and 95° in the shade. In the Periyar valley it varies from 45° to 90°. At the higher elevations such as the High Range, it falls to 25° at night and rises to 50° or 60° during the day. The highest temperature of the air is said to take place in April, when it rises as high as 81°. In December it falls considerably and the lowest heat recorded seems to be 64°. The mean temperature at Trivandrum is 78°.

SEASONS:—This more or less uniform character of the temperature is considerably influenced by the wet and dry weather which marks out the seasons. The dry season commences in January with the commencement of the New-year. It lasts till the end of April. The period of March-April is the hottest part of the year. The hottest portions of the country are in the extreme south and in Shencottah, as also along the ghaut-line. The wet weather begins in about the early part of June and heavy rains prevail till the close of August. The Hindus however, recognise six well-marked RITHUS, or seasons, each covering a period of two months. They are:—Vasanta (Meenam and Medam); Grishma

(Edavam and Mithunam); Varsha (Karkadagam and Chingam); Saral (Kanny and Thulam); Hemantha (Vrichigam and Dhanu); Sisira (Makaram and Kumbam).

DISEASES:—The sudden transition from the cold to the hot season causes, among other diseases fever that claims the largest number of victims. The feverish months are April, May, June, and October and December. The feverish parts are :— (1) the taluqs of Kalkulam, Vilavankode, Neyyattinkarai, Neduvengad, Kottarakarai, Shencottah, Todupuzhai and Minachil; (2) The valleys of the Periyar, Anjanad, Kollasheri, and Idyara ; (3) other parts of forest and hilly tracts. The Sanitary Commissioner of Travancore says that fever, though not fatal, causes, in many instances, such an amount of devitalization that the individuals affected become prone to various intercurrent diseases, unfitting them for the active pursuits of life, if they do not lead to premature decay and early death. Among other diseases prevalent in the country, he mentions cholera and small-pox among the epidemics, and ulcers, anæmia, dropsy, diarrhoea, leprosy, elephantiasis, scabies, yaws or farang worms and dysentery among the sporadic kind.

CHAPTER IV.—GEOLOGY AND MINERALOGY.

We have seen that the country, with its elevations of every variety and extensive sea-coast, with its naked exposure to the violent winds and rain, issuing out of the influence of the Arabian sea, furnishes an interesting field for the study of its meteorology. However interesting the study is, we have refrained from going into technical details. We have, for instance, omitted to discuss the interesting topic of the minor influences that affect the climate, such as the direction of the mountain ranges, the slope of the ground, the nature of the soil, and the degree of cultivation. We have not discussed the relation of Barometric variations to the state of the weather, nor explained why the seasons are reciprocal or of unequal length. We have advisedly left these things out of account, for as observed before we are concerned with only a general description of the salient features of interest and usefulness to the general reader. The same course will be followed in respect of geology. There is an additional difficulty that prevents this subject from a discussion of its technical details. The talented compiler of the "MADRAS MANUAL" rightly observes that the European divisions of the chronological science of geology are ill-adapted for the classification of Indian beds, and even the main names can with difficulty be made applicable. If, as we have seen before, geography describes the design and plan of the world-house we live in, so far as completed, and meteorology records the different processes of water-supply and ventilation, geology discusses its architectural details. It deals with the materials and their arrangements. It is necessary to bear in mind that geologists give the general name of rocks to the several materials such as clay, limestone, chalk, sand, coal, gravel, peat &c., of which the earth-structure consists. The term rock is thus used in a sense wider than the ordinary. The geologists define it as "any mass of natural substance forming part of the earth's crust". The materials of which the earth is built up are called rocks; and the materials, of which rocks are made up are called minerals. The one is geology and the other mineralogy. The two subjects are thus closely allied, and will therefore be dealt with together.

GENERAL.—The geology of the country is more complex and less fully known. Nothing beyond a few scattered remarks is known regarding the state, and the following remarks are taken from the official report of the geological survey of Dr. King whose services were obtained from the British Government to study the geology of the country and examine the thin beds of quartz rocks in the hope that gold might be contained in them. "In the northern part of the country, the mountain mass is very broad, but just south of the

Peermaad parallel, the hilly backbone narrows considerably and becomes a lengthened series of more or less parallel ridges with lower intermediate valleys. These are striking with gneiss, or about west-north-west and east-south-east there being at the same time a line of higher masses and peaks culminating the main ridge, from which the ribs run away, as indicated, to the low country. This narrower and some-what higher land of the west coast presents also unmistakable traces of a plateau or terraced character which is best displayed about Trivandrum, and northwards past Cochin into the Malabar country. Northwards from Trivandrum there are narrow strips of absolutely low land that is on the sea-level, marked by sandy and alluvial flats and long backwaters or lagoons. These widen out northwards from Quilon, until at Alleppy (Aulapulay) there is a width of about twelve miles of such formations, with the very extensive back-water which stretches far past Cochin."

ROCKS :—"THE rock formations are first, and most prevalent and foundational, the gneiss series, and then on it, but only in a very small way, the Quilon beds, which are supposed to be of eocene age. These last are over-lapped by the Varkalai beds, which certainly appear to belong to a different series, and are thus perhaps of upper tertiary age; they appear also to be equivalent to the Cuddalore sand-stones of the Coromandel. Finally, there are the recent deposits. The gneisses are generally of the massive grey section of the series, that is, they are nearest to the rocks of the Nilgiris, though they differ from them in being coarse-grained or more largely crystallized, and in being generally quartzose rocks. The common gneisses are felspathic quartzose varieties of white or grey colours, very largely charged with garnets. A particular form of them is an exceedingly tough, but largely crystallized, dark-grey or greenish felspathic rock. The next succeeding rock formations, namely, the Quilon and Varkalai beds, occur as a very small patch on the coast between the Quilon and Anjengo back-waters. They are said to be argillaceous lime-stones, or a kind of dolomite, in which a marine fauna of univalve shells, having an eocene *facies*, was found, and they occur at about forty feet below the laterite of Quilon, which is really the upper part of the next group. The Varkalai beds, on the other hand, are clearly seen in the cliffs edging the sea-shore, some twelve miles south of Quilon, where they attain a thickness of about one hundred and eighty feet, and have the following succession in descending order:—

Laterite (with sand-stone masses); Sandy clays (or lithomarge); Alum clays; Sandy clays (with sand-stone bands); and Lignite beds (with logs of wood etc). The bottom liginite beds rest on loose white sand, and nothing is known of any lower strata. The recent deposits are the usual blown-sands and alluvial deposits of the low flats along the coasts; an exceptional form occurs at Cape Comorin in the shape of a hard calcareous sand-stone, which is crowded with true fossils and casts of the living *Helix vitata*. It appears to be simply a blown-sand modified through the infiltration of calcareous waters. Loose blown-sands are heaped over it now in places, among which are again thousands and thousands of the dead shells of the past season."

SOILS:—Mr. Logan, in his "District Manual of Malabar", referring to the above report, writes:—"The soils resulting from the geological formations which Mr. King thus describes have been roughly grouped by the natives into three classes, namely:—Pasima (a rich, heavy, clayey, tenacious soil.); Pasima-rasi, (the above with an admixture of sand and of a loamy character.); and Rasi (sandy soils). Each of these classes is again sub-divided into three, so that in reality there are nine classes of soils and this classification is used in determining the revenue assessments on rice lands to which indeed this classification is alone applied."

We pass on to consider the remarkable mud-bank near Alleppy to which reference has been made when describing the coasts. The following is the account given by Mr. Logan in his "Malabar Manual". "The origin of the mud bays or mud banks, which exist at Northern Kollam, at Calicut, and at Narakal in the Cochin State, and at Alleppy in Travancore has never yet been satisfactorily set at rest. The characteristic of the mud banks is that an unctuous mud rises from the bottom of the sea, becomes dispersed in the water and effectually stills the surf. That the mud is always more or less present at the places named is a fact, but the annual churning up of this mud stratum hardly accounts for all that has been observed, and Mr. H. Crawford, the late Commercial Agent of the Travancore Sircar at Alleppy, who has perhaps had better opportunities of watching the phenomenon than any one else, came to the conclusion that subterranean passages or streams communicating with some of the rivers and backwaters, 'become more active after heavy rains, particularly at the commencement of the monsoon, and carry off the accumulating water and with it, vast quantities of soft mud.' In scanty monsoons, the mud banks are less effective as anchorages. He also observed that at seven hundred yards east of the beach at Alleppy, pipes were being sunk at a depth of fifty feet to sixty feet when the shafting ran suddenly down to eighty feet, and several buckets of mud from this depth were brougt up, corresponding in every respect with the mud thrown up by bubbles which he had observed in the sea. A cone of mud, he said, at times appears above the water, the cone or bubble bursts, throwing up immense quantities of soft soapy mud and blue mud of considerable consistence in the form of boulders with fresh water, *debris* of vegetable matter decayed, and is some instances fresh and green. Mr. Crawford's successor at Alleppy, Mr. Rhode, confirms the observation and states that he has seen mud volcanoes bursting up in the sea during the rainy seasons, to all appearance 'as if a barrel of oil had been suddenly started below the surface.' He has come to the conclusion that the mud bank at that place, after being formed in the way above described, is gradually floated away to the southward by the littoral current, and fresh mud banks are formed whenever the hydraulic pressure of the inland back-water increases sufficiently to overcome the subterranean resistance offered by the stratum of fluid mud which exists at the spot described by Mr. Crawford. A further proof, he observes, of the truth of this is to be found in the fact that the extent of mud bank at Alleppy increases and diminishes as the level of the inland waters rises and falls, and this was most observable in the monsoon season of 1882."

MINERALOGY:—Travancore does not supply a good store of mineral wealth. As observed before, the quartz rocks were examined by Dr. King to ascertain if there is any prospect of gold occurring in paying quantities, though, in the neighbourhood of Mlappara, Konniyur and other localities in the hill plateau quartz is said to lie about abundantly in blocks. Dr. King positively reports there are practically no auriferous quartz-reefs, though the quartz itself gives very faintest traces of gold. Iron is abundant, and graphite, lignite, alum, and sulphur also exist. The following account of the graphite working is from the "Madras Manual of the Administration."

"The existence of graphite in Travancore was discovered in 1845 in the gneiss south of Trivandrum northwards as far as Cochin. Some samples forwarded from a locality south of Trivandrum, were considered to be too soft and scaly for the manufacture of pencils, that is to say, by the old method. The martin appears to be a psuedolaterite formed of decomposed gneiss in setin. Samples from this locality and Vizagapatam were exhibited in London at the Exhibition of 1851. An effort was afterwards made to open up one of the deposits and prepare large samples for despatch to London. The situation of this mine was near Ponalur, in the Oolamalcull proverty, about 10 miles north-east of Trivandrum on the road to Arianaud. About 1¼ tons of the stuff were extracted which yielded 1000 lbs., of pure graphite. In all these calculations the estimate of cost at 100 lbs per Rupee at Trivandrum or even less is fallacious, since, it does not appear that the pay for the superintendent of the operations was included in the actual expenditure incurred, nor does it follow that the cost of extracting the out-crop would not be exceeded, when regular mining operations had to be commenced. In 1855 specimens from Travancore, which were laméllar, were described as being soft but brilliant. But the general opinion of experts and manufacturers of pencils in England to whom samples were submitted, was that they were too gritty and impure to be of much value. Samples of a purer graphite have been obtained more recently from a deposit close to Vellanaud, near to Arianaud. The veins in which it occurs are said to cross the strike of the gneiss. Apparently this mode of occurrence, though somewhat unaccountable, has been observed in America also. It is to be noted that the smallest particles of grit in graphite used for pencils is prejudicial, whilst for lubricating purposes, if it is not absolutely pure, it may be injurious to machinery. For the coarser purposes of making crucibles, the presence of iron would diminish the refractory properties of the material. "

Some Mica mines have been laid bare in South Travancore, but none of them are now worked, for no prospect was found of its occuring anywhere in large quantities.

CHAPTER V.—FLORA.

The flora of the state is exceedingly rich and interesting. This is owing to the abundance of hills and forests and to the variety of crops. The hills and forests yield the wild flora, and the cultivated crops contribute to the agricultural productions. We will consider the wild flora first.

GENERAL.—Mr. J. D. Rees hits off most happily the lovely scenery of the Travancore forests which are unique in their own way.—"If the night spent on the way recall the Inferno, the days are those of Paradise when once the hills are reached, and the traveller rides through shady forest under a leafy canopy, only admitting the sunshine by in-frequent shafts; every support of the lofty roof a tall pillar tree with a green Corinthian capital festooned with vines and creeping plants, and the floor covered with an undergrowth of tree-ferns, cycas and flowering shrubs or the graceful cardamom whose smooth glistening oblong leaves wave tremulously in light breezes, which hardly stir the firmer foliage of the trees. Above black monkeys leap joyously from tree to tree; Malabar squirrels jump about, the yellow fur of their stomachs and the red fur of their backs gleaming in the sunshine which catches the taller trees; wood pigeons flit through the sylvan aisles; jungle fowls cackle; woodpeckers tap the tree trunks, and cicadæ shrilly whistle; and yet the general effect is one of silence. In the morning hours one might well call these forests the mysterious temple of the dawn."

Mr. Bourdillon, the Conservator of Forests considers that there is a larger per centage of the land of this state under forests than in any European country or in the United States and says that this peculiarity is undoubtedly due to the climatic conditions prevailing here, the abundant rainfall, the regular seasons, and the equable and high temperature. It is to his exceedingly interesting report which he has recently drawn up on the forest Administration of Travancore in pursuance of the recommendations made by the Commission appointed in 1884, that we are indebted for the following paragraphs on the flora of the country. We should mention also his notes on some of the common trees of the state which are pre-eminent for their utility and scientific value.

Forest Limits.—He describes the forest-line thus:—From Mahendragiri peak it runs east and then south, coinciding with the boundary between Travancore and Tinnevelly. After travelling south for about ten miles, it leaves Tinnevelly and turns west and south-west, following for 5, or 6 miles the foot of the rocky hills north of Aramalay Pass. Still following the foot of this rocky spur it turns north-east and runs for about 5 miles until within a short distance of Anantapuram. From here it runs 4 or 5 miles from north-west, skirting the cultivation, and then 3 miles south-west to near Melapputhur. From here it runs about 7 miles west slightly north, past Vadakur to near Ponmanai. Thence it runs more to the north, and passes over the rocky ridge overhanging Kulshekarapuram (Molagaddy), and leaving Killyurkonam on the left, strikes the Kotha river a short distance above Mayilunni. From this point it follows the Kotha for two miles down to the Arianada dam. The line then turns north-west and runs direct for some 8 miles to Parathipulli (Cocoodi), following the bandy road. Here it leaves the bandy road and keeping to the east of it crosses the Arinada river one mile above the town of that name. It then runs about 12 miles north-west passing Enathi at the distance of a mile and leaving it on the left hand, it runs past Bombayikonum at the the distance of two miles, and then turning due north crosses the Vamanapuram river 3 miles above the town. It then proceeds due north through Kummil and at a distance of 2 miles from Kodakkal, and to the east of it; then crosses the Erur-Kulathuppura road, 2 miles east of the former place; then 5 miles north north-west to the Kulathuppura river, and then for two miles the river is the boundary. The line then turns north-west and Chalakara on the left, runs to

Aunaaycolam, a place rather to the south of Konniyur. From here it goes north, and crosses the Acchankoil river above Kalleli, then north-west 5 miles till it touches the Kallar river, which it follows down to its junction with Rani river at Kumaramperur. From here it goes 10 miles north-west to the Karuvalikkada hill near Alappara and from here five miles almost due north to the Karupalli hill, and on to the Manimalay river. The line then follows the river up to Kannyiappalli. From this place to Erattupetta, the new cart road is the boundary. From Erattupetta, the direction is north north-west for 6 miles to Kayur, and thence north-west 9 miles to where the bandy road crosses the ridge dividing the Palayai and Thodupura valleys near Kilanthara. After crossing this ridge the line turns north-east and passing through Mrala (Mirthala), strikes Udumbannur at a distance of 11 miles, it then runs north-west for 10 miles, and crosses the Vadakkan Ar, 2 miles above its junction with the Shangarapillai thodu. Here the direction is north for 4 miles, the line cutting across the entrance of the Mullaringada valley. From this point, the forest-line runs west north-west for some 20 miles, parallel to the Periyar and at a distance of 4 miles from it, till it is within 3 miles south-east of Malayattur. It then turns north and crosses the Periyar 1½ miles above Malayattur, and proceeds up the Illi thodu,

E.

the boundary between Travancore and Cochin. It then follows the same boundary round to the west for about 8 miles and then proceeds to the Kottassheri river, which it strikes at Erattomukkam on the Travancore and Cochin boundary, after following a winding course for some miles. The northern boundary of the forest area corresponds with the boundary between Travancore and Cochin, and Travancore and Coimbatore. Its eastern boundary is identical with that between Travancore and British Territory, except that a portion of the Shencottah Taluq is omitted as it contains no forest land. The mountainous region enclosed within this boundary measures 3544 square miles and is watered by 18 rivers of different sizes."

FOREST REGIONS.—Mr. Bourdillon divides this region into 4 classes according to their characters, namely—(1) "heavy moist forests of evergreen trees. (2) Land originally covered with moist forest, but now overspread with trees of various ages. (3) Decideous forests with grass growing under the trees and (4) Rock and land covered with short grass and useless for any purpose, except pasture."

FLORA OF THE FIRST CLASS.—"The first class of forests at one time extended all over the low country of north Travancore, but as it covered the best soils it has been gradually cut down there and is now confined to the slopes of the hills and to perhaps one-third of the upper hill-plateau.

The trees composing it grow very close together and exhibit an extraordinary variety of species, and owing to the absence of grass and to the fact that the trees themselves are evergreen, forest fires do very little harm here. In spite of the great choice of woods they offer, these forests are as a rule less valuable than the decideous forests of class III, the greater part of the timber being unknown."

FLORA OF THE SECOND CLASS.—"The second class of forests contains no timber of any value, except Vaga, as the bushes and scrub springing up after a burn are useless kind of trees. All of these bushes or small trees are short-lived and after growing for 10 years give place to better kinds of trees. In this class are included all lands cleared for cultivation of any sort whether for coffee, tea, rice, ragi or other produce."

FLORA OF THE THIRD CLASS.—"It consists chiefly of forest growing on poor land lying at the foot of the hills and is very abundant in South Travancore. These grass forests are found also covering the ridges and higher ground where the soil is too dry for the moist forest to grow. A small part of the hill plateau also is covered with forest of this description. The decideous forests contain a much smaller number of species of trees than the moist forests, but their value is greater."

THE FLORA OF THE FOURTH CLASS.—"Is of course as observed before, worthless as far as the trees are concerned."

In the floral belts described above, flourish the aristocracy of noble trees which supply the most valuable timber, the best Indian fruits and other valuable products. Teak, the monarch of the woods, is found in abundance. It thrives best on the western slope of the hills. About 8000 logs are exported every year to countries beyond the confines of the Indian Empire. The beautiful Anjelly grows in open forests. The Cedar is found on the banks of rivers. The Cinnamon of which there are several varieties, is exceedingly common on hill slopes. The Ebony which is much used for fancy articles, is largely collected at the Shencottah Forest Depōt. The Dammer and Nuxvomica which rapidly attain a great size and give a cool shade, are widely distributed. The Banyan runs wild in the country, and is much planted for avenues along-side of the great southern road. The beautiful Laurel and the graceful Peepul, both held in great veneration by the natives, are found everywhere. Tradition ascribes the abode of Brahma, the Creator, to the root of the Peepul; of Vishnu, the Preserver, to the stem; and of Siva, the Destroyer to the branches. The Blackwood and the Persian Lilac, used much for furniture, rapidly grow up in the Ashambu Hills and the forest glades of Camp Gorge. Cotton occurs everywhere from the sea-level up to three thousand feet. Jack, which yields the most valuable timber, yields no less valuable fruits which are prized much by princes and peasants alike. The Mango, the prince of Indian fruits, is very plentiful, though it is supposed to have been introduced from Ceylon. There are several varieties of which the best is engrafted. The Gallnut and the Gooseberry are very common. Barring the timber trees and fruit trees, the Palm trees are the chief among the cultivated crops that contribute to the agricultural wealth of the country. In the words of an eminent writer, "Travancore yields palms sufficient to give man flour and sugar; milk and honey-like fluids; demulcent drinks and fiery spirits; medicine and soap: fibre for cordage sails and clothing; leaves for thatching and platting, as well as wood for a variety of purposes. Next to the fruit trees and palm trees, rice forms the chief source of agricultural wealth. The rice produced is not a fine variety except in Nanjinaud, justly known as the granary of the south; it is not sufficient to meet local consumption. Next comes pepper, the vine of which grows round the jack and the mango and some of the palm trees which form the main-stay of the poor. It is well-known that the pepper trade of Travancore dates from far beyond the age of Sindbad, the Sailor, and reaches back to Roman times. Within the last few years, Tapioca has been introduced and its cultivation is so extended that it has also become a staple article of food. In the hills, the cardamom which was till quite recently a state monopoly, grows spontaneously in the deep shade of the forests

Coffee has been introduced within the last two or three decades but it does not prosper. Tea takes kindly to the soil. The European Planters make a fortune out of it. Among other productions that consitute the agricultural flora, may be named the plantain, tbe pine-apple, lime, pomegranite, sugar-cane, guava, nutmeg, cloves and other garden crops. It is not therefore too much to say that Travancore is the garden of India.

CHAPTER VI.—FAUNA.

The mountains and forests of Travancore afford some of the best sport to be got anywhere in India, especially in the shape of "large game". The Rev Mr. Mateer says that the sportsman and naturalist will find an endless variety in the fauna—elephants and tigers, for instance, so numerous in some parts that the hill-men are obliged to build their huts on tops of trees—wild oxen and deer, monkeys, crocodiles, snakes, birds, fishes and insects.

GAME LIMITS.—Its northern boundary extends from Pyratumalai north-east along the boundary between Travancore and Coimbatore, as far as the main stream of Paumbar, where the boundary turns southwards. Its eastern boundary runs from the main stream of Paumbar along the boundary between Travancore and British India southwards as far as the pass from Mlappara to Shivagiri, about 10 miles south of Kothamalai. Its southern boundary starts from Shivagiri pass on the east, south-west to the southern-most point of the Paradise plateau. Its western boundary lies from northward along the edge of the cliffs to the Mount Plateau known as Nallathannipara plateau and round its western edge to the Mount Estate and so along the edge of the cliffs to the Granby Estate, the Arathu and the 42nd Milestone cutting on the Peermaad road: thence north and including

Amarthamod: thence along the cliffs including Colahalamed, and again northward along the edge of the plateau as far as Nagrampara, then eastward including Palculamed to the junction of the Mothirapara river with Periyar: thence to Munaar on the High Range and thence including all land above 400 feet and running west of Anamudi along the western edge of Hamilton's plateau and across the valley to Vyrathumalai. (Vide Govt. rules).

"GAME".—Includes bison, sambhur, ibex, mouse-deer, hares, deer, jungle-fowl, peafowl, quail and such other birds.

CLOSE SEASON.—The Regulation for the preservation of games provides that it shall not be "lawful for any person to shoot at, kill, capture, sell or pursue any of these animals during specified periods and any female or immature male of bison and ibex at any time except for the protection of life or of crops or produce."

OTHER WILD ANIMALS.—Elephants whose ivory is a source of State Revenue, are numerous. Tigers, leopards, bears, horned antelopes, porcupines and monkeys of varied species are common. Elephants are abundant all along the Western Ghauts, especially on the Anamalai Hills, named so from that circumstance. It is one of the oldest known of animals. At a very early period, elephants were used in war by the Indian nation. They are captured by Government establishment. Some are taken in pitfalls dug for the purpose. Some are driven into large enclosures called Keddahs. They are also captured by female decoys taken out for the purpose. A herd of elephants is always led by a female, never by a male. They are largely used for the transport of timber from forests to river-banks. As a badge, the elephant represents the Chera and the Chola dynasties. It is the emblem of the Royal House of Travancore.

DOMESTICATED ANIMALS—Of these, the cattle are the most important but not peculiar to the country. The Vetchoor cows find much favour with the people and enjoy a high reputation for yielding maximum profit for minimum expense. Goats thrive well. Dogs and cats are reared in homes.

AMPHIBIOUS ANIMALS :—The most conspicuous among these are the crocodiles and alligators which infest, in large numbers, the lakes, canals and rivers.

FISHES.—Different varieties of mackeral, perch, sardines, shark, herrings, sunfish &c abound in the backwaters and the sea. Fishing is carried on by nets, by hoops and by poison.

BIRDS:—The stork, bittern, pelican, teal, and several species of aquatic birds are abundant. The peacock, quail and other birds haunting the woods, are unparallelled for the beauty of their plumage or the wonderful sweetness of their music.

INSECTS.—They are represented by different varieties of beetles, bees, wasps, ants, moths, grasshoppers and locusts.

REPTILES:—Snakes of various species are abundant. The chameleon, the lizard, the flying dragon and others of the kind are also numerous. Of snakes, however, the country is the seat and centre. They are held in great veneration by the people. A corner of the compound of every wealthy Tarawad is set apart for the abode of snakes. These abodes are called Kavus or serpent-groves. There are thousands of such groves in the country. Idols of snakes are put up there on a stone-basement called Chitrakoodam. Periodical offerings are made and considered essential for the prosperity of the household.

The People.

CHAPTER I.—THEIR EARLY MOVEMENTS.

Of the original inhabitants we know very little. They have to be looked for among the Hill tribes who are supposed to be the aborigines. They are aboriginal in the sense that their settlement was antecedent to the ordinary population. They number between 8,000 and 10,000 persons, and are split up into 12 or 14 tribes who dwell apart in isolated tracts. The KANIES inhabit the patches of forest about the basin of the Paralai, the Kothai, the Ney, the Vamanapuram and the Kalladai rivers. The PALLARS are found along the neighbouring woods of the Kulakada and the Atchencoil rivers. The MALAYADAYARS, called also Moodavanmars, frequent the hill-fastnesses of Nanattapara, Chengamanad and Neriyamangalam. The HILL PANDARAMS live in caves found along the mountain-course of the Pamba. The KOCHUVALENS occupy the forest regions lying along-side of the Ranni. The ULLADANS tenant the elevations round which winds the Palayi river. Along the foot of the hills from the Periyar to Thodupuzhai, the ARAYANS (known also as Vailanmars and often called Mala-Arayans or Lords of the Hills) are scattered in numerous camps. They and the Uralies in large numbers wander over the Thodupuzhai Hills, and were at an early date the property of the Alwancherry

Thambrakal, the recognized chief of the later Numboory immigrants. The Cardamom Hills near Vendametu form the habitat of the PALLIYARS. The MANNANS are most numerous on the hills east of the Periyar up to the foot of the High Range, while the slopes of the High Range contain the bulk of the Muthuvans.

Of these tribes, the last three speak a language more akin to Tamil than Malayalam, and freely inter-marry with the Tamils. They have, therefore, probably immigrated from the Tamil country. Mr. Munro states that Mannans are said to be descended from men of various trades in the Tamil country, and on certain days do Puja to the tools of their ancestors. They claim superiority over the other tribes and are tall, sturdy and pleasant-looking. Formerly, they appear to have been numerous, but are now fast decreasing in strength.

The other tribes have sprung from the original inhabitants of the country. They are dark-skinned, short-nosed, thick-lipped, and possess the worst features of all. Their ancestors probably betook themselves to the forest to escape from the yoke of slavery under which their Pulaya congeners of the East Coast languish even to this day. They speak Malayalam and are broken up into numerous knots or *Kudies*. They do not intermarry. Each village has its own headman. Among the Muthuvans and the Mannans, the leadership is hereditary. The produce of the wilderness and the spoils of the chase afford maintenance to the majority of them. Some, however, own patches of cultivation and raise plantains, tapioca, yams, chillies, etc. They are excellent trackers, expert in clearing paths and invaluable as guides to travellers. They are employed to gather honey, dammer, ivory, cardamoms &c., for the forest Depôt. They are demon-worshippers. They assign to every grotto a genius. In every leaf, cabbage or herb, they fear injury is concealed. They are afraid that these evil spirits may emerge out of darkness and swallow them up. On this ground, many pieces of forest are left uncultivated, while the land in the neighbourhood has been reclaimed.

Besides the jungle tribes who wander over mountain fastnesses, those brought under predial bondage by the successive waves of immigration go under the generic title of CHERUMAR. This class is represented by the Pulayas, the Pariahs, the Vedans and the Ulladars, each of whom, influenced by the prejudices of caste, is spilt up into distinct clans. Though the yoke of hereditary slavery has been removed, they, as a class, still remain in abject social degradation. They are distinctly Dravidian without fusion as the Hinduised castes are with fusion. They comprise about a tenth of the population and are probably one race of unmixed blood. They constitute a distinct ancient race which has its own subdivisions, its own traditions and its own jealousy of the encroachment of other low castes. They are by occupation the servants of the Nair agriculturists. They are settled in remote huts and left wholly to nature. They are very industrious and faithful to their masters. They gradually push their way to a better position. The Christian Missionaries admit them to equal rights and privileges in Mission Schools and Churches. The hill men and the Cherumars represent the hunting and the pastural or agricultural tribes. They used to labor under many and vexatious disabilities and disadvantages which however have gradually been removed. Gratuitous service of various kinds used to be exacted from them. They had to guard Sirkar properties, to work in Sirkar forests in cutting down or transporting timber, and to carry Sirkar things from place to place. Families of these low castes were even allotted to certain private individuals who were at liberty to obtain gratuitous service from such families. Then again, there were many restrictions placed on their personal liberty. A proportion of low castes was indeed subject to avowed slavery. As such they were attached to lands like chattels and were bought and sold. Their masters were authorised themselves to punish them for refractory conduct, a power which it may be imagined was frequently abused in no small degree. Even those that were not avowed slaves used to be treated almost as such. They were not at liberty to keep cows,

They could not use oil mills. They were interdicted from carrying on trade. They were debarred the use of any but coarse cloths. It is improper in them to wear any but the most ordinary personal ornaments whether males or females. It was not open to them to decorate sheds erected on marriage occasions. They were restricted to particular music. They were denied permission to move in conveyances. They could not even wear shoes or use umbrellas. It was considered improper to allow them to use metallic utensils. They could not build substantial or tiled houses. Nor could they acquire landed property with impunity. In fact these unfortunate low castes used to be treated as quite an inferior order of creation and were endlessly or hopelessly exposed to misery and degradation.

Now all these things have been put an end to by Government notification or by being allowed to fall into deseutude. They enjoy now the same amount of personal liberty and protection as the high castes. The influence for good of this fair treatment has been most marked. There are now 892 schools for the benefit of these classes and Government have established 170 scholarships to encourage learning among them. The policy of the Maharajah has been all along to deal equal mercy and equal justice to all.

The first wave of immigration brought the

cultivators of the palm trees. They bear different names in different parts of the country. In South Travancore and on the other side of the Ghauts they go under the name of SHANARS; in Central Travancore they are known as ILAVAS; in North Travancore their designation is CHOGANMARS; in Malabar they are called Tiyas; and in South Canara, BILWAS is the name—a slightly modified form of the term ILAVA. Their name is commonly derived from a root, meaning an island and the common tradition is that they immigrated into the West Coast from Ceylon. Mr. Stewart, the Superintendent of the Madras Census of 1891, thinks that probably the connecting link between the word "Dweepam" and "Tiya" survives in the caste name "Divas", which is returned from South Canara. In support of this theory Bishop Caldwell, the great Missionary-Scholar of South India, observes that the general and natural course of migration would doubtless be from the mainland to the island, but there may occasionally have been reflex waves of migration even in the earliest times, as there were certainly later on, traces of which survive in the existence, in Tinnevelly and the Western Coast, of castes whose traditions and even, in some instances, whose names connect them with Ceylon. They forced the earliest tribes to keep moving on, when they themselves came to be pushed from behind by fresh-comers. Their hereditary occupation is palm-cultivation and

H.

toddy-drawing. The majority of them confine themselves to the labour appointed to the race; but a considerable number has taken to agriculture or trade. They reduced to slavery the remnants of the vanquished aboriginal tribes. The Dravidian demonolatory is retained by them. Of all the Indian tribes, they number most converts to Christianity. They are a hard-working and industrious people. In them is to be seen the best type of the peasant population. They have advanced at a pace which puts to shame their congeners of the East Coast. They now form a solid community which has by strenuous efforts been released from the bondage of centuries. Large numbers of them now represent fair culture. Some are authors; others take to medicine; some are editors and others again hold Government offices in the country. On every side there are signs of active advancement and no pains they spare to prove themselves eminently fitted to enjoy the rights and blessings of freedom and right citizenship.

CHAPTER II.—THE NAIRS.

The next wave of immigration brought the Nairs of whom Sir. W. W. Hunter records that for ages they were "hereditary warriors" and appear as a military nobility in the early Portuguese records of the 15th century," and that they are now distinguished alike for their success in their intellectual professions as barristers, judges and administrators and for their manly vigour in arms. They have always been essentially a martial people and form a distinct race of compact nationality, having in their manners and customs little or nothing in common with the Tamils of the East Coast. They appear to have entered Malabar from the north and were probably the off-shoot of some colony in Konkhan or Deccan. The Tiyas who moved by the S. W. and the Nairs who have found their way by N. W. passes appear to have converged and crossed each other in Central Malabar, as the Dravidians and the Colarians and Tibeto-Burmans have done in Central India in the early movement of the Indian races. The Nairs who, like the Dravidians, proved the stronger, broke up the Tiyas and the mass of the earlier tribes whose scattered fragments, like those of the Colarians and Tibeto-Burmans, were thrust aside to mountains and pathless forests. Like the Dravidians, the Nairs rushed forward in a mighty body and formed a huge and permanent settlement. Though they were subdued by the higher civilization of the later Brahmin immigrants they were never broken up. They willingly associated themselves with the Brahmins. And this intermingling of the races has been felicitous in its results.

The Nairs are serpent-worshippers; they hold serpents in great veneration, and a corner of the compound of every wealthy Taravaud is set apart for their abode. There are thousands of such groves or KAVUS in the country, and the worship of the serpent-gods, deemed necessary for the affluence and prosperity of the house-hold, obtains to the present day. Within the limits of this sacred grove, serpent-idols are put up on a stone basement called CHITRAKUDAM built for the purpose. These idols are propitiated with periodical offerings, by the eldest female member of the house, of NEERUM PALUM, that is, an ambrosial compound made up of flour, milk, water of the tender cocoanut, fruit of the KADALI plantain, ghee and honey. On such occasions, the Valluvar or the kurup sings and dances.

The Nairs live in series of scattered home-steads or farms and are very religious. The heart leaps up when one passes by a picturesque Nair house at even-tide and hears the inmates utter "RAMA, RAMA," in pious devotion.

They are hereditary warriors. Their warriordom is attested by their civil organisation. In former times each petty Rajah under the great Swarupam of Rajahs ruled his own portion of territory, designated a Naud, and was named NAUDUVAZHI. He was not considered a Nauduvazhi who had not at least 100 Nairs under him. Next in rank were some other still smaller rulers called DESAVAZHI (the military chief of a Desam).

The number of Nairs or fighting men attached to him was from 25 to 100. Subordinate to the Desam came the Tara. Subdivisions of the Tara were TAWERIES. A Taravaud corresponds to what the Romans called a GENS, with this distinction that whereas in Rome all the members of the GENS traced their descent from a common ancestor, in Malabar the members of a Taravaud trace their descent from a common ancestress. The large Taravauds set apart property for the common use. Any number of private families may be comprised in the Taravaud. Every member of a Taravaud has an equal share in the common stock—the infant as much as the aged. No member can claim his share, but the Taravaud as a body can make such division as it pleases of the common stock. When partition takes place, the Taravaud becomes cut up into as many Taravauds as the members may have settled to form among themselves. In the Taravaud the entire property is managed by its senior member or KARANAVAN for the benefit of the whole family.

He becomes head by birth and resembles the father of a Brahmin family in respect of his rights and obligations. He has equal interest with other members and is the guardian and representative, for all purposes, of the property of every member within the Taravaud. He should decide what family ceremonies are necessary. He cannot renounce his rights and as the head of the family, has entire control over the property. He may assign it for maintenance. He may delegate and resume management. He may resume property allotted for maintenance or before proceeding otherwise he may narrow his rights. He can hold private property,, but is incompetent to alienate the Taravaud property, without the consent of the other members, except to supply its necessity or discharge its obligations or for its benefit. He is removeable for mismanagement, for extravagance, for disregarding family interests or for incapacity, but not for any single act of of misfeasance. If removed, he is eligible for maintenance and cannot be replaced by a stranger.

All Taravauds follow the Marumakkathayam law of inheritance by which though the property is held in theory to vest in the females only, the males and females have equal right. Practically the males are co-sharers with the females. Under this rule of nepotism a man's property goes to his sisters; sister's sons; sister's daughters; mother; mother's sisters; their children;

maternal grand-mother; her sisters and their children.

The origin of this system has given rise to inaccurate notions and gross misconceptions.

The stupid notion gratuitously sought to be pitchforked into general currency is that in view to preserve the family property intact, and to let it descend undivided, the Namburies or the West Coast Brahmins permitted the eldest son alone in their family to marry; that the remaining sons, if any, were obliged to form temporary alliance with Nair women; that the children of these alliances being illegitimate tho *descensus a matrice* or matriarchal system of inheritance came into vogue. But how ridiculously, absurd this notion is, will be abundantly manifest from the historical fact that the advent of the Namburies was long after the settlement of the Nairs in the country, and that generations and generations of Nairs must have inherited, acquired, enjoyed and passed property before. Intense ignorance or melancholy malignity has gone even so far as to reproachingly ascribe this system of inheritance to uncertainty of parentage. These in the hands of unenquiring commentators has, in the words of Mr. Logan "brought much obloquy on the morality of the people. The fact at any rate of recent years is that although the theory of law sanctions freedom in their marital relations, conjugal fidelity is very general. No-where is the marriage tie, albeit informal, more rigidly observed or respected, nowhere is it more jealously guarded or its neglect more savagely avenged. The absence of ceremonial has encouraged the popular impression, and the ceremonial like other conventionalities is an accident and Nair women are as chaste and faithful as their neighbours."

Let us investigate the subject impartially and dispassionately so far as is within the scope of this chapter. As explained before, the Nairs appear in early times as a military nobility. They were hereditary warriors and protectors of the realm. The system of Kalari which was originally organised to impart to every Nair instructions in the art of warfare, continues here and there even to this day. According to this system every Nair of a certain age was, like the early Spartan youth, bound to undergo training in arms and serve as a soldier whenever wanted. The process of training was known as ADAVU and each batch of the ADAVU class consisted of 200 men and more. Such batches were numerous. Experts among the trained men were put at the head of the Militia. The Nair lords and noblemen of those days correspond to the barons and knights of early England. The VIRUTHI system, abolished only within a few years of late, was little short of a Royal grant for the maintenance of the militia, since those were days marked by an ever-waxing, never-ending, clannish clique and struggle for power and supremacy, which constantly required the services of the military sons of the soil. The humiliating reluctance which the Nairs felt accordingly to leave their property, in time of war, to the rude shock of continuous neglect or outside forces and influences, naturally induced them to have recourse to a judicious arrangement which made the descent to run in the female line. The daughters thus became the darlings of the race. This arrangement gave women considerable influence: admitted of their being, to some extent, educated; and saved them from the pressing privations of Brahminical tyrannical widowhood. The matriarchal system of inheritance thus owes its origin among other things to the constitution and condition of the Nair society in the early times, the peculiar system of land tenure then in vogue and to the genius of the Government of the ancient Rajahs. Mr. Logan says that "this system was adopted to prevent alienation of property, as the earliest foreign observer Sheikzin-Ud-din himself sets forth."

Certainly there is much to commend itself in the alienation of property which, no doubt, the system tended to prevent,, but that was only an effect that followed from *and not the cause* of the arrangement. Mr. Logan himself adds that" the system had also much to commend itself in a society organised, as it then was, when the *nairs were the Protectors of the state and could seldom except in old age, settle down to manage their town affairs.*"

Thus it will be seen what michievous meddlesomeness and blatant blunder it is to connect the system of marriage with the system of inheritance and to make the one the inevitable incident of the other.

It is this self-same blunder that has led to reflections on the morality of the people—reflections based on inaccurate notions which the excusable ignorance of carly European travellers and writers, who have had neither a long stay in the country nor acquintance with the language of the people nor even, owing to caste-restrictions, free admisson into their society, has largely but wrongly ventilated. The magnitude of the mischief that such enormons statements are calculated to bring upon the people, can be fully gauged when we reflect on the unfortunate circumstance that these erroneous statements have found favour with jurists and adminstrators of law. Neverthless it goes without saying that, if to err is human, it is man's privilege to correct the error.

In a clear, careful and clever speech before the Travancore Legislative Council, in introducing a Bill relating to marriage among the followers of the matriarchical system of inheritance, the late Mr. P. Thanu Pillay the learned mover of the measure, goes deep into the question of the *essentials* and *accidentals* of human marriage and comes to the conclusion that the good faith and the intention of the parties and not the form in which a marriage is celebrated, is the test of its validity; that the existing social marriage among the Marumakkathayan Hindus is, *in all essential respects, a valid marriage*; that only legal effect has to be given to what is already recognised as valid; that a community should be judged by the usages of the good men that compose it and not the waifs and strays in it, and that if one would cast off all prejudices and pre-conceived notions and impartially and dispassionately investigate the subject, he will find the conjugal union known as SAMBANDHAM or PUDAVACODOOGA or by the other local names, is not a casual or fugitive connection formed for the purpose of sexual gratification, but a serious and solemnalliance, and that the intention of the parties is to make the union a life-long one.

Ceremony, publicity or solemnity is not wanting either. The noticeable features of a Nair marriage are the preparation of the *Mukurtha-Charthu* and the formal settlement of the wedding day by the ceremony known as *Ashtamangalyam*; the fixing of the main pillar of the wedding hall and the putting up of the *Kathir-Mandapam* on an auspicious day; the procession of the *manalan* or the bridegroom-elect who should be from well recognised families, called *Machambimar* and who, in the part of the country between Edavai and Padmanabhapuram, were, for each Kara or village, appointed by royal writs; the tying of the Tali amidst acclamations of approval, known as *Kurava*, the giving of *Ayanioon* and *Boothakulam* or *Bumper* feasts to the bridegroom's party, a custom believed to be a relic of the encampment of the Mohamedan army at Manakaud; the *Vathalthura* songs and amusements; the procession of *mannuneerkonduvarica*, with pomp and music and the like. This is just like any wedding in Brahmin life and is, when the girl attains age, followed by *Pudavaicodukka*—a ceremony analogous to the sacred *Rithusanthi* of the Brahmins. For this also the castemen and relations reassemble and the important thing is the gift of a cloth by the husband-elect to his lady-love, in token of their conjugal alliance. Nair-women giving birth before publicly and openly taking a husband in the manner above described are put out of caste and held in utter reprobation. In the face of these customs, exclaims JUSTICE RAMACHANDRA IYAR, "How can one say there is no marriage among the Nairs. There is no truth in the general condemnation that the ties of marriage are not respected in Malabar. It may be observed that *constancy of love and attachments to one's husband are virtues as much respected among Nairs as among any other community*".

We have entered into the questson at this length, since it deals with a matter of unique socialogical interest and in view to present a faithful picture of the civic life of a much-maligned but progressive South Indian Race. It is an encouraging feature of this progressive Nair Society of to-day, that not-withstanding their sub-divisions into castes and sub-castes—such as the CIREATHILL NAIR or the house steward who held, in times of yore, high offices in the Covil and military services of the country the ILLAKKAR or tenants attached to Branmin Illoms; the SORUBHAKAR rendering feudal service in Kshatria families; the PADANAIR or the warrior clan; the MANAVALAN or the cultivating branch; the PALLICHANAIR or the bearers of the palanquins of the prince and chiefs &c., &c., :—that not-withstanding such innumerable social and racial barriers, the community, as a whole, is adapting itself, with remarkable alacrity, to the altered conditions engendered by contact with the progressive civilization of the West.

A FAIR DAUGHTER OF MALABAR.

(From a picture by Mr. Ravi Varma).

CHAPTER III.—THE NAMBURIS

The Brahminis came next. They come under two broad sub-divisions namely, the Malabar Brahmins or the Namburis and the East coast or Dravida Brahmins.

We shall deal with the Numburi Brahmins first. In simplicity of manners and general truthfulness of character, in reverence for time-honoured customs and unostentatious zeal for religious devotion, the Numburis are as a rule scarcely excelled by any other class of Hindus. They are said to have been brought over and settled by Parasurama. The legend of Parasurama is not of any great historical significance except perhaps in two ways. In the first place, the people believed and largely used it in their literature. In the next place it is a fanciful version of dim memories of the early settlement of the Brahmins and the civilization they brought with them into the new land. The name of Parasurma is used to give a fanciful explanation of the way in which the greatest Aryan tribes reached their final home in Southern India. The Brahmins like the Dorians were much too proud a people to own the truth that they had been pushed southward from one halting place to another by the pressure of the stronger tribes in their rear. The Dorians preferred to call their arrival in Peleponnesus the return of the children of Heracles. Like-wise the Brahmins preferred to call their arrival in Malabar the return of the darlings of Parasurama who had made a gift of the land to them, and to think that they were only called back to their rightful heritage.,

They soon founded villages and temples and began to exercise a powerful influence at the court of the Malabar kings. In the early hisory of the Namburi castes we find a division into two parties namely the Punniyur congregation following the Vishnavite faith and the Chovur faction adopting that of Siva. The latter finally prevailed and has since been incorporated with the Vedanta Doctrine of Sankaracharya, himself believed to have been a Numburi. The organization of the Numburis is by Gramas or Villages, as that of the Nairs is by Taras or lands. The Numburi community of the present day is split up into two religious factions namely, the Tirunavai group and the Trichur league, each presided over by a Vadhyar or high priest. The highest order of the Numburis is called the Namburipad or one who has performed a public sacrifice. The illustrins house of Alvanchery Tamprakal stands foremost in rank and exercises to this day the right of ministration on the coronation day of the rulers of Travancore and Cochin. Eight such families of religious reputation exist to this day under the name of AshtagrahatilAdhyar. These eight families are Poovalli ; Uzhappamun ; Varikkacherry ; Kadalur; Purayannur ; Oralacherry Mepad ; and Edamana. Besides these there are certain classes of Numburies who have forfeited their original status on account of their having pursued [callings independent of the study of the vedas. Such are the physician Namburies known as Ashtagraha Vaidyar or eight familes of physicians who having from ancient times devoted themselves to the study of medicine are recognised and resorted to by the people as hereditary physicians. Such are again the soldier Namburies called Sasthrangakars who constituted the ancient militia of 36000 men named Rekshapurushas or protectors of the realm. The Sasthrakali or performance with swords and shields obtains to this day. Such are also the Sankethika Namburies who, not prepared for the initial troubles incidental to colonisation, went back to the land they came from, but returned when order was restored and peace began to reign. Under this class are included the Tiruvella Desis or those who betook themselves to the place of that name and and the Karnat and Tulu Desis who immigrated to the southern districts. Such are some of the main divisions of the Namburi classes of today. Sir Seshia Sastri hits off most happily the leading traits of this class of people when he writes. "The proud Namburi Brahmin land-lord who traces his ancestry and his tenure through several thousands of years and whose anxiety to preserve the dignity of the family is indicated by the strict law of entail by which the disintegration of his property is prevented, is yet a victim of indebtedness caused chiefly as elsewhere by the variously expensive character of the marriage of his daughter and by his unbounded charity and hospitality."

The Namburis are extensive land-owners often possessed of immense wealth. The family property is owned and enjoyed in common by all the members of family. Division of family property is forbidden. It is rarely or never practised. The law of inheritance is makkathayam by which the makkal or sons are the legal heirs of a man's property. But the estate is cut off from all the heirs-general. The eldest son alone inherits his father's wealth. Others merely claim support from him. Those who can claim such support are the males of the family, their wives, their virgin daughters and widows while residing in the house. Owing to the expensive character of marriage which is due to the practice of making large endowments to the bridegroom as well as to the anxiety to let the property pass undivided, the eldest son alone is allowed to marry. If he be without issue, he may marry one to two additional wives. If the eldest brother still have no children or die without issue the next in succession may marry and so on. When the family is in danger of extinction, it is the common practice to give the daughter of the house in marriage to a Namburi and to take him into the Illom which is the house name of the Namburis. This is known as "Sarvasvadham" marriage according to which the whole estate of the father-in-law passes after his death to the management of his son-in-law. He is moreover disentitled to property, if he fails to beget any issue. This is peculiar to Namburis alone, Adoption is also made to perpetuate a Namburi family in the following three ways; I., "Patukayyil" adoption or one in which five persons take part. II. "Chamathu" adoption in which a pan of sacred twigs of *Ficus religiosa* is burnt. III. "Koodivachu" adoption in which a surviving widow or an old man adopts an heir by merely taking him into the house. Mr. J. D. Mayne says that the last form of adoption obtains in the Mithula country under the name of krithrama adoption. The women of the Namburis are called antharjanams or inside folks. They are guarded with jealousy. The institution of caste investigation or a Court of enquiry in case of adultery; the terrible method of pronouncing sentence against an adulteress, the disposal of children after guilty career; the ordeal that suspected persons have to undergo; their loss of caste and social position; all this unmistakebly proves the exalted importance with which chastity among other virtues is reckoned among them.

Among other social peculiarties the following are said to have been inculcated by Sankaracharya:— "It is declared that all unmarried women among the

Antarjanams who die, are not to be burned without the ceremony of the Talle which ceremony must be performed by hired Brahmans. Without this it will be an abomination.

"In an Illam (or house of the Numburi) no Karmas are ceremonies are to be performed without the attendance of a Sudra; therefore it is decreed that in all Illams Sudras must be employed as servants to the Numburi.

"It is decreed that none but the genuine Brahmans of Kerala alone are permitted to enter into the Ambalam of a Devasthanam where the God is placed. The Antarjanams, Ambalawasi girls and Sudras only are to have access to the Sannidhi and all other inferior castes are strictly enjoined to stand without at certain distances according to their several distinctions of caste and profession.

"It is decreed that Illams and barnams (the house of the Sudras) must not be constructed so as to form regular st eets and lanes but they are to be scattered and every individual is permitted to build at his own convenience and pleasure.

Brahmans alone are permitted to sit on boards formed in the shape of a tortoise shell and it is decreed that if any of the other castes are found to use such boards as seats, they will be liable to be capitally punished.

"It is decreed that Sudras in their barnams or houses who have a desire to keep their favourite deities as objects of their adoration must have Brahmans at least once or twice in the year to perform certain ceremonies."

With reference to the sixth law allowing the younger sons of an Illam to perform connections with Sudra women it is decreed that the latter are not considered pure.

"It is decreed that Brahmans are prohibited from the observance of one of the six actions or Karmas called bhikshadanam by which they are restricted from the practice of receiving alms.

"It is decreed that the Rajastries of the Kshatriya tribe or pure Brahmans alone may cohabit with them, and eating what is cooked by these women in their house will not be considered an abomination.

"It is decreed that Brahmans have the right of preventing a Raja or prince of the country from putting any individual to death, and his right is derived from a pre-eminenee of holding the birth right inheritance as a gift from Parasurama."

"It is decreed that a Brahman must wear unbleached cloths whilst performing the office of Karma among them; otherwise it would be an abomination."

"It is decreed that it is not considered a violation of the law for a Brahmani woman to marry. after she attains the age of puberity."

"It is not considered impure for a Brahman not to clean his teeth or for him to let his nails grow to aprodigious length, nor is it uncomely for them to shave every part of their body with the exception of the hair on their head."

"It is an not objectionable thing for a Brahmin to eat of the pickle made by the Ambalavasi and Sudra castes, and the parpadas or light fired cakes, made by Konkanies and Kshatriyas."

"Besides the Brahmans, all other castes of whatever description, are expressly forbidden to cover the upper part of their body above the navel."

"Brahmans, Sudras and other castes indiscriminately are forbidden to wear a covering on their head or a covering to the foot."

"It is decreed by these precepts that the regulations of the Brahmans are never to be altered."

These social rules and regulations of the Namburies distinctly mark them out from the *Dravida Brahmans*, who came next into the country.

CHAPTER IV.—DRAVIDA BRAHMINS.

The West Coast Brahmins came next. The lovely aspect of the country, the humane Government of the Maharajahs, and the easy and peaceful life of the people made Travancore highly inviting. The peace-loving Brahmins found in the happy valley of Travancore ample scope for sweet communion with the most High. The liberal patronage which all branches of knowledge were sure to find in the Court of Travancore was not the least inviting. The unflinching liberality and the free feeding of the state give them complete relief from the worry and trouble of life on the East Coast. The cheap living and the peculiar social customs of the people allured many into the country. The extensive tracts of lands which only waited to be touched by the hand of man to smile on him with plenty, the natural richness of the country and the never-failing monsoons also formed a powerful charm. As soon as peace was declared from one end of the country to the other and the charity the Maharajah made known by the opening of free feeding-houses, a regular exodus from the east began in right earnest. The Brahmins who are unnecessarily stigmatised as an inordinately home-loving class, shook off all ancestral considerations and repaired in large numbers into Travancore. Since then, small colonies of Brahmins have been settling down about the

Dharmasalas, and many new villages have sprung into existence. A fresh impetus was given to the inland trade with the East Coast. The ruined merchant, the impoverished land-lord, the bereaved widow, and the helpless orphan—all found in Travancore their only hope and means of living.

They are divided into :—

Tamil Barhmins ; Telugu Brahmins ; Mahratta Brahmins ; Kanarese, Brahmins, and so on according to the country they have come from and the language they speak. Each of these is split up into subdivisions according to their religious faith. Of this we shall speak later on in the section treating of Hinduism. The Brahmins were hereditary priests. Learning was, as everywhere in the early times, their monopoly. They had absolute power in the promulgation and elucidation of ancient law. The Indian arts and sciences were the fruits of their sole devotion to the progressive state of mankind. Religion, society and literature were the powerful manifestation of their extraordinary intellect and benevolent activity. They accomplished most of the purposes of writing by their remarkable memory which is now considered one of the most wonderful feats of intellectual gymnastics. They were in brief Apostles of Hindu culture and Hindu progress. Of them, the late Sir. W. W. Hunter, the most historical voice of the Century, writes thus:—" The Brahmins were a body of people who in an early stage of this world's history bound themselves by a rule of life, the essential precepts of which were self-culture and self-restraint. As they married within their own caste, begot children only during their prime, and were not liable to lose the finest of their youth in war, they transmitted their best qualities in an ever-increasing measure to their descendants. The Brahmins of the present day are the result of three thousand years of hereditary education and self restraint, and they have evloved a type of mankind quite distinct from the surrounding population. The Brahmin is an example of a class becoming the ruling power in a country not by force of arms but by rigour of hereditary culture and temperance. One race has swept across India after another : dynasties have risen and fallen : religions have spread themselvcs over the land and disappeared. But since the dawn of history, the Brahmin has calmly ruled, swaying the minds and receiving the homage of the people and accepted by foreign nations as the highest type of Indian mankind." Hence the potentialities of the new education will not fail to incline the modern reader with indulgence towards the following exalted appeal which learning is said to make to the Brahmin: "I am thy precious gem; preserve me with care: deliver me not to a scorner and so preserved thou shalt become supremely strong." (Chapter II 114). Cordially accepting the service which he was thought fit to own and discharge, the generous Brahmin set himself to the performance of his sacred trust and founded to the best of his opportunities, a glorious specimen for the collection and diffusion of the highest kind of knowledge. He distributed life based on the elaborately organised system of rituals and ceremonials promulgated in the Vedas. Four stages have to be gone through by every Brahmin in his period of existence. The first which is always binding is 'Brahmacharyam'—student life—for which all ages of civilization and progress are equally and eminently conspicuous. The initiation is inaugurated with elaborate religious ceremonials. The investiture of the sacrificial cord is considered one of the most essential of the purificatory rites to be gone through by the pupil before entrance into the regular course of vedic study. The investiture comes off between the 5th and 6th year of one's age beyond which he is said to lose his position in life. By the performance of this ceremony known as 'Upanayanam' he becomes twice-born and qualified for admission into the Hindu convents and sacred academic groves. The Vedic studies are pursued only for 6 months of the year. For religious purposes the year is divided into two periods:—the 'Uttarayanam' period which is the half-year in which the sun moves from South to North (summer solstice). (2) and the 'Dakshinayanam' period which is the half-year in which the sun moves from South to North (winter solstice. Of these the former is regarded as inauspicious for the study of the vedas. All Brahmins close their vedic studies on the first full moon day of the "Uttarayanam" period and commence vedic studies. This is known as "Upakarma" which obtains to the present day. The young men girt with the thread used to leave their houses and go off with their preceptor to live with him and learn the sacred scripture, by submitting themselves to a regular course of discipline. The first and the most important lesson impressed on them is the due recognition of the highest place in our nature which reverence most magestically claims to occupy. Every Brahmin student is taught that "By honouring his mother he gains the terristrial world by honouring his father the intermediate or the ethereal world; and by assidious attention to his preceptor the celestial world of Brahma (Chapter VI 253)" To dismiss the mythological figure, he is taught above all that reverence is the highest duty—a lesson of the highest moment and virtue.

Having learnt the lessonsof the Vedas and thus formed a high conception of duty, the Brahmin is naturally prepared to fight out what the late poet laureate Tennyson calls the healthy breezy battle of life. He enters on the stage of "Grahastasramam, or Married life and settles down as a citizen.

What strikes at once even the most casual observer is the absolute absence of the separation of families. All the members of what is known as a natural family., live in a common dwelling with exclusive privileges and extensive powers, liable to the control of the *pater familias.* who is bound to maintain them all out of the family property under his control. Every son when he arrives at a marriable age and accepts a suit puts his claim to provision for his newly married wife as he does not, like his occidental brother generally go off and live in a house of his own. Every daughter, when she is given in marriage, stands and insists upon her rights to dowry from the common funds. After her marriage she becomes subject to the control of the family into which she is married.

The whole family moves at the concert of the chief who keeps all the members under his rule and orders. He is the sole presiding agent of every detail of domestic duties from observance of daily rituals and the distribution of food to the discussion and solution of weighty problems affecting the weal of the whole family. He gives the finishing stroke on all occasions of note and his authority is beyond question. He is the benign satrap of each family and looked up to by every member of it with little short of reverence and awe.

The reason for this is not far to seek. Look where we may in the annals of nations, we find everywhere that vast authority and great dignity are placed in the noted wisdom and ripe experience of age. The dangerous and designing Cassius who dreaded the power of the eloquence of Cicero was tongue-tied with the assurance by Decius Brutus of the hope that his silver hairs would purchase him a good opinion and buy men's voices to commend his deeds.

The eminent Sir Henry Maine goes even so far as to think that " there is s Survival of this idea in the minimum limit of age which has been made the condition of a seat in the artificial second chambers which have been constructed over most of the civilized west as supposed counterparts of the English House of Lords. While so how could not have the authority of age made itself the ruling authority in those days when the people had to seek ingenious means to hand down to posterity the rich heritage of their traditions, for want of a common medium of lasting communication.

Its application to the family seems further to be based on due and clear recognition of the healthy principle of one supreme power in a small group of individuals bound together by family ties. There is yet another and a stronger reason why the Aryan religious tenets favoured it. And that is the consideration for the helpless widows, the worn out old men, and the sportive and careless children to all of whom alike the conditions offered by the joint family system have been and are found indispensable in all stages of social evolution. Thus grew amidst the Brahmin the system of joint family life *paripasu* with married life or life of a citizen. After the accomplishment of wordly desires in the above order of life and consequent achievement of self control and self discipline, he redeems himself from the domestic bondage and passes through the 3rd order of an anchorite in the forest.

Preparing himself thus for the 4th and the last order of "sanniasin" or asceticism, he relinquishes everything worldly and consecrates himself to purely religious musings for the attainment of heaven and happiness "When thus he has relinquished all forms, is intent on his own occupation and free from other desires, when by devoting himself to God, he has effaced sin, he then attains the supreme path of glory."

Such in brief is the fourfold basis of perfect life according to the conception of the Brahmins. Of these the first and second orders of life appear to wear on their faces unmistakeable marks of time-proof durability. The confirmed craving for the growth of human intelligence has placed the working of the first on a vast and gigantic scale, and it is being sufficiently encouraged and developed to its full extent by the consecrated energy and enter prise of our Western friends and benefactors. The traditionary principle of the maintenance of the race has thrown the second order also *terra firma* as the first. The distinct maintenance by the high authority of Vasishta and Boudhayana, of the optional tenor of the four orders, coupled with precedent and usage, not to speak of the claims and demands of a later age, has resulted in the decay of the last two orders. The proportion of the forest recluse and the ascetic is fast going down, although the spiritual tendency of the Brahmins generally still remains stationary. The present creed gives every Brahmin the dignity of the unit. He has the glory to take a road of his own. He may live out the life of a student and bring all the forces of his culture to bear upon the extension and amelioration of his people or he may remain to the last a citizen enjoying the sweets of personal and social life or according as he likes may retire into proud and pious isolation or work out his spiritual benefit.

This completes the circle of the leading Hindu sections of the population. We shall deal with the non-Hindu portion of the population in a separate chapter. We cannot bring this to a more fitting termination than with a few general observations on the dominant characteristics of the natives of this State. Without any the least fear of a charge of inordinate love of race we may call to witness Lord Connemora, a former governor of the Southern Presidency of Madras who bears unmistakable testimony to the natural and high-bred courtesy which distinguishes the natives of this State. We may add from intimate personal knowledge, that this courtesy is not of the formal kind. It readily and cheerfully responds to the call of help. Even the poorest Hindu tries to render what little help he can. He requires no concerts, no associations, no subscription lists or anything of the kind in aid of charitable purposes. He does not require the painful appeals of actual distress and suffering, such as are the direct incentives to action in other countries. To him the begging Pandaram is no less an object of pity than the helpless widow and orphan The religion in which he lives, moves and has his being enjoins on him to do deeds of charity for its own sake. He plants trees by the roadside, builds wayside inns, sinks wells, digs tanks and affords very many facilities for the rest and refreshment of the way-worn traveller. In all seasons and at all times, he seeks to mitigate the sufferings of his fellow men. In fact in no other country in the world can be beheld a similar spectacle of private charity. We indulge in no language of false patriotism or rhetorical flourish when we record the bare fact that the Maha Rajah is a worthy representative of his people and deservedly bears the glorious appellation of Dharma Rajah on account of his traditional benevolence and far famed charity.

CHAPTER V.—LANGUAGE AND LITERATURE.

An ethnological account of the people should not lose sight of their language and literature. Malayalam is the language of the people. This is better localised than any of the languages of South India. It is spoken in the south of Canara, throughout Malabar, in Cochin, and in Travancore. It is spoken hardly at all elsewhere. The Malayalam-speaking population amounts in all to four millions in the Madras Presidency, including the native state of Travancore and Cochin. Those who speak it are chiefly Hindus. It is also spoken by the Jews, Mahomedans and Christians. The language is peculiarly related to Tamil. Some scholars think that it is an off-shoot of Tamil; others ascribe to it a Sanskrit origin. There is yet another school of opinion which holds that like Tamil it is an off-shoot from the original parent stock of Dravidian languages. However it be, there is no doubt about its close affinity to both Tamil as well as Sanskrit. It abounds in rich and elegant expressions from Sanskrit. Its idioms bear a close affinity to Tamil. The history of the Malayalam language begins with Ramacharitham, the oldest Malayalam poem still in existence. Composed as it was before the introduction of the Sanskrit Alphabet into the Malayalam Language, it deserves well of the particular attention of scholars.

With the arrival of the Brahmins, the great ardour for literary pursuits began. As the Nairs formed the Military sons of the soil,the art of archery and swordsmanship was taught to every Nair. Every Nair of a certain age was bound to undergo training in arms and serve as a soldier, whenever wanted. The process of training is called Adavu and each batch of the Adavu class consisted of 200 men. Such batches were numerous. They were the guardians of peace. There are several works on the subject. But the best that I have seen is a stout MS. copy secured in the Palace Grandha Library, Trivandrum. It gives an elaborate and vivid description of the use of arms, designs of fortresses and bastions and carrying on of intricate and important military campaigns.

MALAYALAM MEDICINE. The Travancoreans developed also the science of medicine, It formed the special subject of study to the members of eight families of the Namburi immigrants. They are known as Ashta Vydiar. In some places they are called Nambian or Nambi. In other places they bear the name of "Moos". Medicine like Astronomy was an independent development in the country. The Namburis explored and studied the original works in sanskrit such as the "Nidanams" of Madhavcahari, the "Ashtanghridaya" of Vakbhatachari, the physiological works of the celebrated Susrutha and the materia medica of the eminent Charaka. They became very skilful in medicine, diagnosed and treated diseases and performed surgical operations wonderfully well. In course of time they themselves produced original works in Sanskrit which can be had now.

There is however no knowing when and by whom they were composed. However, as will be seen later on, these works have been done into Malayalam. Although originally the study of Medicine was prosecuted exclusively by the Namburis, the Ambalavasis, an intermediate class who were versed in Sanskrit, came to be initiated into it. They in turn taught the subject to the neglected Nairs. And since the language of the latter is solely Malayalam, the Sanskrit works written by the Namburis were first translated into Malayalam. Dr. Gundert appears to have collected a good many of them and used them largely in the compilation of his valuable and voluminous Lexicon. These prose renderings seem to have been put into verse by several scholars subsequently. Of the "Ashta Vaidyans", Kuttanchery Moose was an eminent physician. In this family was found a malayalam translation of the great medical work known as "Sahasrayogam." Allatur Nambi, another physician of repute is said to have written "Roganidanam". The "Yogamritam" which is said to be the work of a Numburi of Triparayar, deals with the process of preparing drugs out of minerals and stones. "Vaidyamailka," is a very useful and important publication. It is a source of considerable help to native medical practitioners

MALAYALAM ASTRONOMY. Astronomy also formed a subject of special study and interest. Like Indian Astronomy it is the subject of admiration in respect of observations made. It is also the object of contempt in respect of its degeneration first into Astrology and then into the "Mantravadams" of Malabar.

The exigencies of the national worship gave a great impulse to the Numburis to learn to calculate the solar year, the phases of the moon and the disposition of the stars. They wrote original works based on the production of the Sanskrit Varahamihira and Aryabhatta and other writers on Indian Astronomy. One Namburi whose name is unknown wrote the "Tantarsangraham"; another who is familiarly known as Vadacherry Namburi was the author of "Jatakapadhathi". A third has composed a gloss on the above. This is the beginning of Astrology. And in course of time the "Brahmajatakem" of Varahamira was translated; as also the "Lilavathi" and "Prashnareethi". The last mentioned is the great work of Talaculathoo Battathiri. Several original works were also written in Malayalam.

MALAYALAM Law also engaged their close attention. It has been rightly observed that the first step towards the state of a civilised society is the protection of the right and property of persons. It is very gratifying to find that this most important measure has engaged the full attention of the original adminstrators of the realm. Major Walker, in his exhaustive report to the Madras Government on the land tenures of Malabar, puts on record "that in no country in the world is the nature and species of property better understood, or its right more tenaciously maintained than in Malabar." This is quite as true in Travancore. In this country, as in Malabar, possession of land originally was unalienable, and confined to Namburi Brahmins. There are two treatises on Malabar law: (1) Vyavaharamala & (2) Vivada Ratnakarum based more or less on the institutes of Manu. Dr. Gundert appears to have consulted the Malayalam renderings of these works. These works were probably written when the power of the Brahmins began to decline and the petty chiefs and the children of the soil commenced to rise to importance. *Ankam* and *chunkam* were the two methods by which offenders in those days were punished. They deal with Criminal and Civil offences respectively. According to Ankam a person guilty of an offence is branded with a mark of degradation and sent away. He would be an object of contempt and warning wherever he goes. And that was considered a severe and sufficient punishment in ancient times. The method of chunkam required that an offender should take an oath on a Palli Ambu or the bow of the Divine Rama. The bow would be planted on the ground and the person who has, for instance, failed to pay a debtor or Government tax would have to swear by the holy bow that he would pay off the dues within a certain date. The faith of the people in the evil effects of an oath unfulfilled or broken was in those days as it is even now, so strong that the chunkam method bound them sufficently to discharge their obligation.

MALAYALAM EPICS. The great bulk of Malalam literature consists of translation or adaptation of the great Indian Epics of the Ramayana and the Mahabaratha. Thunchathu Ezhuthachan who flourished in the 17th century is the father of Malayalam literature. He was the first to introduce into the language its modern alphabet of the Grantha characters. He wrote several works which are at this day read with pleasure and profit. He has impressed on them the forms of Kilipattu harmony—a species of composition supposed to be sung by a parrot. This literary artifice answers to Milton's "Sing, Heavenly Muse" or "Descend ye Nine." The Ramayana, the Mahabharata, and the Bhagavata of Ezhuthachan belong to this species of composition. They are his best works. It is a mistake to suppose that his works are translations from the Sanskrit. No doubt he has drawn largely upon the rich lore of the great Indian Epics. But his consummate judgment in the selection and arrangement of the materials, his original reflections, and his copious, pure and eloquent expressions have infused into his works a fresh soul of harmony. He is allowed the same rank among Malayalam poets as Virgil among the Roman and Homer among the Greek.

MALAYALAM LYRICS. The first and the best of the Malayalam lyric poets is Kunjan Nambyar. Gifted with talents of a high order, he has invented a new type of National lyric, called "Thullal" of which the subtlity and pathos are eminently suited to the genius of the language. The merit of the Thullals lies in their simplicity of structure, in the delineation of character and in the fineness of sentiments. Of this species of poems he has a large number which will live and rouse up genuine interest as long as the language endures. The Thullal poems are more or less based on the incidents which fill the episodical portion of the Mahabharata. Another kind of poetical composition which has immortalized his name is Manipravala or poems in which the elegant pearls of the sanskrit phraseology are interwoven with gems of native expressions. Among recent original productions, "Mayur Sandesa" or the peacock messenger by that Sanskrit savant—the Valia Koil Tampuran is a rare ornament to this class of composition.

MALAYALAM DRAMA. The spirit of the Malayalam drama is illustrated and summed up in what is known as "Katha kali." It has the nature of a pantomime but the actors never speak. The play is represented by mute action or dumb show, while the text will be vociferously sung by a party of musical experts. As the curtain rises, the several actors enter the stage and translate into the language of finger-signs and other variety of show, the sense of the dramatic entertainment. The science of symbols has attainted to a high state of perfection. The Maharajahs of this country used to take a special interest in *Katha Kalis* and have themselves composed several plays of this kind. The Maharajah who died in 973 M. E. and his brother Aswati Thirunal, the Kottayam Rajah and the Kottarakkara Rajah were poets of repute in this kind of composition.

Of the new type of the drama, Kerala Varma Valia Koil Thampuran is a great ornament. This scholar of rare attainments and culture, to whose self-denying earnestness and unremitting labours, the Malayalam language owes so much, has given a turning point to the structure and history of the Malayalam drama by his first and unrivalled translations of Kalidasa's matchless production of Sakuntala, Of this undisputed literary lord of the Malayalam country, Sir George Wolseley wrote thus in an issue of the *Leisure Hour* :—"I found Mr. Kerala Varma, husband of H. H. the Maharajah's elder sister, a particularly interesting man to talk with. He is a Fellow of the Madras University and a Member of the Royal Asiatic Society, well-informed, very intelligent and exceedingly courteous in manner and address very like H. H. the Maharajah in that respect." The sanskrit model thus introduced was quickly followed. From this time the art made great and rapid advancement.

Latterly Justice Mr. Govinda Pillai has introduced to the Malayalam-speaking public the type of the English Drama by his translations of some of Shakespeare's immortal plays. The new turn of poetical composition he has contrived to employ is the first specimen of Malayalam blank verse which, at the touch of the magic wand of gifted genius, bids fair to become the ground-work for the noblest poetry of the Malayalam tongue.

MALAYALAM NOVEL. This species of composition is of recent origin. The first Malayalam novel after the model of Sir Walter Scott is "The Marthanda Varma." Its gifted author displays in this work a singular acuteness in penetrating into the secret springs of policy and motives of action. He has cleverly pieced together the fast-dying fragments of legends that gathered about the revered name of Marthanda Varma who, in the early days of the baron's wars, had like Robinhood wandered *incognito* through the forest glades of south Travancore. In "Akbar" by the Valia Koil Thampuran, we have specimens of the pathetic, the descriptive, the eloquent and even the sublime. The novels of Chandu Menon have decidedly a ring of Lord Lytton's wonderful works. "*Induleka*" which has the rare merit of being done into English by Mr. Dumergue is remarkable for the purity of its diction, tenderness

KERALA VARMA, C.S.I.,

Valiyakoil Tampuran.

of its sentiment and the light it throws on Malabar manners and customs.

MALAYALAM LITERATURE. Though the language is indebted to a foreigner for its first grammar and lexicon, the history of its literature is first produced by a native to whose talents and perseverance it bears unmistakeable testimony.

Dazzled by the multiplicity of striking objects which actively shape and illumine contemporary literature, the pioneers of literary advancement in this country formed in 1891 a literary congress for the enrichment of Malayalam literature. With it new thoughts rose in the people's hearts. Every department of letters began to be actuated by a spirit of progressive activity. The variety and abundance of works produced in a few years are eminently marvellous, With the composition of the "Kerala Paniniyam" the language has received a new lease of life. The "Bhasha Bhushan" by the same gifted writer is the first treatise on Malayalam rhetoric. The appearance of the Introductory and Chemistry primers in Malayalam marks the beginning of scientific literature embodying modern science and modern thought. The translation of Dutt's "Ancient India" and other publications point to the progresss in historical literature. The ennobling patriotic impulse and unwearied industry of Scholars are fighting against all odds to enrich the Malayalam literature. We earnestly commend to their praiseworthy endeavours the necessity of issuing a collected edition of the works of the leading poets of the land. We think this will receive the willing patronage of His Highness the Maharajah whose greatest pleasure is to encourage learning in every possible way. It is well known that the Royal House of Travancore has all along been a Royal house of many literati. It is to this day remembered that the throne of Travancore was once graced by a sovereign whom the general consensus of the age regarded as a marvel of learning and who was therefore styled *Sakala Kala* Marthanda Varma or Marthanda Varma who is learned in all the arts and sciences. As Padmanabhapuram was the capital of the country, a shrine appears to have been erected there and dedicated to Divine Saraswati, the Goddess of learning. All the Maharajahs used to visit the temple and do service every day. And since the Maha Rajah now holds court in Trivandram, the image of the Goddess is taken to Trivandram once every year and special pooja or worship is done on a grand scale. The literary eminence of the court is still maintained.

Religion and Caste.

The principal religion professed by the people are Hinduism, Mohamedanism, and Christianity. Budhism appears to have flourished formerly in the country.

HINDUISM. The bulk of the people profess Hinduism which is the State Religion. Here too there was a memorable struggle for supremacy between the Church and the State. But things took a different course. While in Europe the State triumphed, the Church in Travancore as in India acquired a monopoly of influence. The dedication of the whole state by the great Rama Varma in 925 M. E to Sree Padmanabha, the Guardian God of the land, and the assumption of sovereignty by him as *Sree Padmanabha Dasa* or the vicegerent of the deity (a title retained to the present day) afford a striking proof of the State being absolutely subservient to the Church. In connectiou with the annual Oolsavam or festivity celebrated in that memorable shrine of national service, we have a symbolical and concrete illustration of the above, when H. H. the MahaRajah with the sword of fealty in hand leads the Aurat procession attended by the officers of State and the Knightly barons of the soil. Even today the popular belief is that a portion of the *Vishnu Kalai* or the halo of Divine Vishnu hedges round the king. With the accesion of the church influence, the Brahmins became potent factors in the evolution of Hindu society. Their influence palpably coursed through the entire extent of the land. In the words of Mr R. C. Dutt it moved round in a series of concentric ripplets on the placid surface of the society, expanding from the inmost circle of the Brahmins and gradually dying away to the furthest extent. The different classes of the society thus live as though in the life of the Brahmins. Hence Mr. Nagam Aiyah is quite right when he wrote in the last Census Report that Hinduism is perfectly synonymous with Brahminism and means and includes all the articles of faith of the orthodox Brahmins.

ITS THREE-FOLD WORK. In Travancore the work of Hinduism is *threefold.* Its *religio-social* influence has given rise to the caste organization of the people. The purely *religious* aspect of it deals with the maintenance of the State Church and attempts to solve the problem of death and afterwards. Under its *socio-religious* aspect it has organised a system of charity, private, state-aided as well as state-assumed and has so far successfully grappled with the problem of the poor—a problem which at all times, in all societies and under all Governments is a source of considerable trouble and trial to the State. We shall afterwards have occasion to notice this portion of the subject in connection with State Religion and State help. We would therefore turn our attention here to the first two aspects alone.

CASTE. As a social organizer Hinduism recoginises that in the social world, diffused power cannot be made to work. A head of water or a store of heat or electricity is more useful than a level ocean of water or diffused heat of the earth. Hinduism saw clearly that difference of level was as essential in the working of the social organization as in the physical world. It attempted to preserve the social vitality and found it necessary therefore to prevent the absorption of growing Aryan civilization from its less civilized non-Aryan surroundings. The irresistible ascendency of the Brahmins gave them a vantage ground which they were not slow to utilise. The result was that " the several orders of an industrial society has got fossilised in course of time into rigidly exclusive castes ".

ITS UNIVERSALITY. Mr. Wilson says in his work on Indian castes " that the system of caste was not the growth of a single age or even of a few centuries" and adds " pride of ancestry of family and personal position and occuption and of religious pre-eminence, which is the ground characteristic of caste is not peculiar to India. Nations and peoples as well as individuals have in all countries, in all ages and at all times, been prone to take exaggerated views of their own importance and to claim for themselves a natural, and historical and social superiority to which they had no adequate title. " In illustration of such inequalities we may point to the aristocracy of blood in England, the aristocracy of culture in Germany, the aristocracy of wealth in America. They demand an etiquette of difference between the varied communities of the world. They are founded on distinctions and differences caused by the conditions of social evolution—conditions which in our country grew up under the powerful and pervading influence of religion—conditions whose inviolability has been the means of preserving to us intact for ages and ages together the indelible land-marks of our social architecture. Mr. W. S. Lilly remarks:—"No doubt all members of the human race are equal as persons but with this equality co-exist vast inequalities arising from the degree of personality and the conditions in which it exist." Dr. Lorimer in supporting a similar position asserts in his excellent work on "Studies in social Life" "We cannot entirely destroy social inequalities even if we would. Their real foundation is not property but humanity. To abrogate them we must abrogate man and that is plainly inpossible". We strongly deprecate therefore the uncharitable spirit not infrequently displayed by our critics whose comments tend to widen the gulf already existing between class and class. We are not oblivious to the evils of the system but what we contend is that the eradication of such social barriers is a grand work of *compromise and conciliation.*

ITS ARRANGEMENT. A few of the divisions and

sub-divisions of the people have already been incidentallly referred to in the preceding pages. Others of them will be here noticed. We arrange our notice of them in an order which is convenient for treatment but which has absolutely little to do with their social position or precedent, our object being merely to give the reader a general idea of the excessive complexity of the system and the principles of classification on which it is based.

CHAPTER I.—HINDUISM (SOCIAL.)

THE BRAHMINS. As observed in a previous chapter, the Brahmins of Travancore come under two classes:—the Dravida Brahmins and the Malabar Brahmins. The Dravida Brahmins are divided into five classes. The Tamil Brahmins alone strictly belong to the Dravida group. They comprehend the *Smartas* who follow the teachings of Sankaracharya; the *Vira Vishnavas* who are followers of Madwacharya; the *Sri Vaishnavas* whose religious leader was Ramanuja; the *Bhagavathas* who with equal favour look upon the worship of both Siva as well as Vishnu; and the *Saktas* who worship *Sakti*. Turning to another principle of classification, the Tamil Brahmins are divided into the *Vadamas*, or the north country Brahmins; the *Madhyamas* or the middle country Brahmins; the *Sankethis* or those who in ancient times formed a miscellaneous clique of their own and so on. Dr. Hunter says that the Dravidians have been settled in organised masses from the dawn of history down to the present day and the present Revenue system of India is still founded on the old Dravidian Revenue system which grew up thousands of years ago.

THE MAHRATTAS form the next group of the Dravidian Brahmins who have come from the country of the Mahratti language and who have played a prominent part in the Political history of Travancore during the last century. When H. H the present Maharajah was presented with an address by the Members of the Madras Mahratta Association early in December 1888, H. H. eloquently remarked in warm appreciation of their services :—"Your kindly regard for the ancient principality which men of your nationality have naturally helped to make it what it is, has again manifested itself by the cordial welcome you have given me on the happy occasion of my present visit to the city." They are divided into several Sub-castes such as the *Desastas* who count among them the greatest of the Marathi bards; the *Konkanasthas* or the *chit pavanas* to whose order belong the famous Peishwas; the *karhadas* who are said to have been made by providential Parasurama and who have produced the great Marathi poet Moropant; the *Kanwas* who represent the "first Sakha of the whole yajur Veda" and are numerous in Kolapur; the *Madhyandinas* to whose community belong the family priests of the Raja of Kolapur; the Padpas who are teachers of the tribes found in the highland above Konkan; the *Patashas* who are priests, physicians, astrologers; the *Kirvantas* who are cultivators said "to have sprung from twelve Brahmins"; the *Trigulas* whose occupation is to plant the piper betel ; the *Javalas* who perform menial services connected with hearth of Brahmins; the *abhiras* who "act as priests, herdsmen and cultivators"; and others too numerous to mention. Thirdly there are the Andhras or Telinga Brahmins who speak the Telugu language known as the Italian of the East. Referring to the sweetness of their language, Dr. Wilson quotes a verse which runs as follows:—"The Marathi is sand; the Turuku (Hindi) is dust: the Kanadi is musk; the Tenugu (Telugu) is honey; the Oda (Odra) is strength".

The Telugus are cut up into numerous castes. The *Vaduasalus* and the *Kamamkulus* belong to the Rig Vedic group. The *Murukanadus*, the *Nyogis* and the *Madhyandinas* profess the Yajur Veda. The *Madwacharyas* and the *Ramanujas* follow the teaching of their respective religious leaders. And last not least we have the Karnataka Brahmins who have their own sub-divisions, and the Konkani Bramins who are scattered over the whole tract extending from Goa to Cape Comorin.

MALABAR BRAHMINS. There are eight classes of them to whom reference in detail has already been made elsewhere. The offsprings of Namburi Brahmins by Kshatriya women after the extirpation of all the male members of the Kshatrya community, are known as Koil Tampurans. Since they are allied to the Royal House, we shall have to advert to the subject again under that head.

Besides those already mentioned there are several intermediate classes:—

(1) There are the *Adikals.* These are Worshippers of Bhadrakali and exorcisers of spirits. They wear sacred thread. They follow be Nepotismal law of inheritance. Their women are known as Adiammamars. To them seclusion is unknown. The taluq of Thiruvalla is their chief habitat.

(2) *The Pushpakan* is another class whose occupation is temple service. Some of them follow the patriarchal, while others the matriarchal system of inheritance. Among the former, the dowry of a woman goes to the family of the husband, if it is undivided, and to her alone, if divided. The sons inherit the property of both the mother as well as the father. In default of sons, the grandsons, if any, do. In default of them, the brothers and their heirs inherit the property. Even among Marumakkathayi Pushpakans, property is bequeathed only in the absence of sons.

(3). There are again the *Nambis* who are teachers in the art of Kallari or archery and swordsmanship.

(4). The *Plapallis* are those who supply flowers to temples. These two classes are found in 23 taluqs.

(5). The *Psharadis* are said to be descendants of the Brahmin who, while almost prepared to the order of asceticism, relinquished it, owing to the lifelong privation it entailed. As an indication of this, they bury their dead with salt—a practice common among sannyasis alone. They do not wear thread. Their occupation is service in the temple.

(6). *The Varyars* are another class found everywhere except in the frontier taluqs of the South and East. They are governed both by the matriarchal and patriarchal system of inheritance. Among the former class, one distinguishing feature is that division of property is allowed.

(7) The *Chakyars* or those who chant the words of God are found in the eight taluqs north of Karunagapalli. Their women are called Nungiars. They sound the cymbal when the chakyar performs his *kooth*—a kind of monodrama based on the Indian Epics. Their entertainments are held in seasons of temple festivity. Among them the nephew and not the son inherits property.

(8) There are again the *Nambiars* who also take part in the performance of the chakyars. They beat the drum. They do not wear thread. They marry Nangiar women and are governed by the *descensus a matrice*. It was the indignity cast on the Nambiar class which induced and inspired the great national poet of the country, himself a Nambiar, to compose a new species of dramatic entertainment known as Thullal. This has been already adverted to.

(9) *The Thiyatunnis* form another class. They are exorcisors of spirits, worshippers of sylvan gods and oracles of their Divine Majesty. They inherit both from father to son and from uncle to nephew. They wear thread.

(10) *The Kurukkals* are seen everywhere. They are numerons in the north. They wear the sacred thread. They supply flowers &c. to temples. They inherit from uncle to nephew.

The Malayala Sudras go under the name of the Nairs—an indication of the military nobility to to which they belonged. They constitute the main portion of the population. The majority of them are agriculturists. They are tenants of Jenmis whom they treat as their liegelord. Among them there are 18 sub-divisions.

(1) *Kiriyathil Nair* :—These are known by the names of Kuruppu, Nair, Kimal, Menon &c. They enjoy many privileges. They are great landlords They held in former times important places in the Government Service. They were ministers, commanders of the army, chancellors, and Sthanakanakus.

(2) *Illkars*. They bear the names of Tampi, Kurup &c. Originally they were tenants attached to the rich Namburi illams.

(3) *Swarupakars*. They had in former times rendered feudal service to the several swarupams or Kshtria families of the Malabar Rajahs.

(4) *Padmangalams* serve in the pagoda.

(5) *Tamulpadoms* follow a variety of occupations. The social barrier among the abovementioned five classes is very light and being fast swept away. Any of these classes can by Royal Nit or by adoption become entitled to the privilege of the highest class. Only it has to pay Adiyara or Commission fee. The women of the family so raised in status may thereafter interdine and intermarry with the members of the higher classes. With the advancement of civilization the adiyara restriction is fast dying away.

(6) The *Edacherry* Nairs, called also Pandaris, are engaged in tending cows, selling ghee &c.

(7) *Marans* are known by different names in different localities. They are known as Oachen, Marayakurupu, Mangalyam &c. &c. They are employed in the pagodas. Their general occupation is beating the drum. They are governed by the Marumakkathayam law. They are found in almost every taluq. Large numbers of them live in Mavelikarai.

(8) *Karuvelattu Nairs* are supposed to have been brought here from Kolattunad when a member of that family was taken to the Travancore Royal House. They serve in the palace as custodians of the Maharajah's Jewels and valuables. They are found most in Kappiara and Thiruvattar.

Besides those enumerated above, there are the Olattu Nair, Pallichan &c. &c. They are merchants, weavers, washermen and artisans. Among the artisans there are six classes: Asari (carpenter) and Musari (brazier), Kallasari (stone-mason), Thattan (goldsmith), Kollan (Blacksmith). Similarly amongthe lower classes there are several sub-divisions. The Paraya and the Pulaya are original races peculiar to this coast. They are useful and hardworking. They work in the fields and are found in every Taluq. They number the largest converts to Christianity. Such are some of the several layers of which society in Travancore is constituted on the caste basis of Hinduism.

CHAPTER II.—HINDUSIM (RELIGIOUS).

Hinduism as observed before is a religious confederacy. It represents the coalition of the Vedic Brahmins with the ruder rites of the lower castes and tribes. It is a religious federation based on worship. As the race elements have been moulded into castes so the old beliefs and religious elements have been worked up into gods. Hence we find the pagodas in the country divided into two classes, those dedicated to superior Divinity and those dedicated to inferior Divinity. There are 6159 pagodas of the former kind and 3205 of the latter out of a total of 9364. The higher castes of the Hindus worship the higher Divinity. Of the temples some are under Government management while the rest belong to corporations called Ooranmakars. These are of 4 classes :—(1) Ancient temples said to have been founded by Parusurama (2) Temples founded by Rajas. (3) Temples founded by communities or leading individuals. (4) Temples founded by sannyasis or ascetics. The manager of a temple of the first two kinds is called Devaradi Ooralen or manager subordinate to the Deity, while in the last two classes he is called Ooralaradi Devan. These are institutions of a by-gone age. Graem says that the general superintendence of all endowments vested in the sovereign and was termed Melkoimma which meant nothing more than the right of ruling power to interfere in the case of disputes or fradulant practices occurring and to remove and appoint trustees at his pleasure. The subjugated barons of Travancore exercise such a right by the appointment of Koimmas.

Ooralan is the name of the manager whether he is appointed by the king or the founder of the institution or the founder himself constituting the manager. The officers subordinate to an Ooralan are four in number:—

(1) The *samudayam* or persons appointed by an Ooralan as his agent to manage the affairs of the temple. This office is hereditary and liable to be dismissed for misconduct (2) *Santi* is the person employed to perform puja or service in the temple. He is appointed for a certain term at the discretion of the Ooralan.

Kazhakam is the menial servant whose function is to keep the pagoda clean and supply flowers for daily worship. This office is generally appropriated by the classes of Psharadi, Variar and Numbiar.

(4) *Pattali* or rent-collector is also a paid servant of the Ooralen.

Any servant of the temple who holds hereditary right for this office is called a *Karalan* and he is said to possess *Karaima* right. His office answers to that of a Mirasikarnam in a Zemindari. The Ooralers are the proper persons to sue and be sued as representatives of the temple. They have a right to alienate trust property but they can create subordinate tenures. They have no power to alter the constitution of trust. The number of Ooranmakars varies in different places.

The Travancore temples are known for their antiquity, for their religious sanctity, for the excellent scenery of their sites and for their architectural beauty. It is unnecessary and cumbersome to give a detailed description of the daily service, festivals &c in Hindu temples. The Hindus like other nations worshipped first as they feared, then as they admired and finally as they reasoned. Their earliest Vedic Gods were the stupendous phenomena of the visible world. The deities became divine heroes in the epic poems and legends and they were spiritualised into abstractions by the philosophical school. The world-renowned Sankaracharya (himself born in Travancore) has moulded the later philosophy for us into its final form and popularized it as a national religion. In the words of a great native Scholar of Indian as well as European History, " from land's end to land's end he traversed the continent ; wherever there was an opponent, he was ready to meet him in argument he—the Aristotle of his age—brought all the forces of his masterly dialectics to bear on the subject, over-throwing all opposition and converting all to the cause of god and of holy writ. " He addressed himself to the high caste philosophers on the one hand and to the low-caste multitude on the other. He has left behind him as a two-fold result of his life-work (1) a compact Hindu sect and (2) a popular religion. Siva-worship he introduced as a link between the highest and the lowest castes. Vishnu worship supplies a religion for the intermediate classes. Siva-worship combines the Brahminical doctrine of personal god with the Buddhistic principle of spiritual equality of man. These worships furnish a religious bond among the Hindus in the same way as caste supplies a social federation among them. In the words of the late Sir Monier Williams "it is a remarkable characteristic of Hinduism that it neither requires nor attempts to make converts; nor is it by any means at present diminishing in numbers, nor is it at present driven off the field as might be expected by being brougnt into contact with two such proselytising religions as Mahomedansim and Christianity. Another characteristic of Hinduism is that it is all receptive, all comprehensive. It claims to be the one religion of humanity, of human nature, of the whole world. Hinduism has something to offer which is suited to all minds. Its very strength lies in its infinite adaptability to the infininite diversity of human characters and human tendencies. It has its highly spiritual and abstract side suited to the philosophical Brahmins; its practical and concrete side suited to the man of affairs and the man of the world; its aesthetic and ceremonial side suited to the man of aesthetic feeling and imagination ; its quiescent and contemplative side suited to the man of peace and lover of seclusion. Nay, it holds out the right hand of brotherhood to fetish-worshippers, nature-worshippers, demon-worshippers, animal-worshippers and tree-worshippers."

CHAPTER III.—BUDHISM.

In its conflict with Hinduism, Budhism offers to the student of history a very complex but instructive problem. Synchronous with the caste organisation of the country and the growth of the power and influence of the Brahmins, Budhist and Jain missionaries spread over this coast. Mr. Logan thinks that the flight of the 1st Brahmin immigrants from the country *for fear of serpents* contains a reference to the Jaina immigrants whose symbol was a hooded snake. But he is in error when he conjectures that the Perumauls were originally of Jaina pursuation. We find that the Perumal invited six Brahmin apostles to meet the Jainas in argument and to over-throw their influence and power. Bhattacharaya, Bhattabana, Bhattavijaya, Bhattamayukha, Bhattagopàla and Bhattanarayana were the apostles and they brought all the forces of their dialectics to bear upon the subject and converted all to the cause of the Hindu Triad. ***Sasthrakali*** or a species of worship peculiar to this country is the sole product of their triumphant compromise. The object of the worship is to seek protection from the attacks of the snakes. The Deity worshipped is *Sastha*, the Divine offspring of Vishnu and of Siva. There were originally 18 congregations set apart for the worship. A lamp is lit up and four Numburi Brahmins are seated round. They tell *Manthrams* in praise of the Deity. This is followed by songs some of which are a withering piece of satire directed towards the aggressive faith. Here is the substance of one of the songs:—"Can an elephant be killed by bugs ? Can the mountains find wings to fly with? Can two rats plough the wide expanse of the world-encircling ocean ? Then can Hindusim be supplanted."

The Brahmin apostles settled themselves permanently in the country, The Perumal honoured them with large *Kizi* presents and made endowments of lands measuring to the extent of 5000 *Kalan* seed-capacity. Their sandals were also preserved as a mark of honour. Despite the iconoclastic work of the Brahmins to reinstate Hindu gods in the Budhistic temples, there are still relics of their being originally places of Budhistic worship. The temple at Chitral in South Travancore is one of the several instances in point. It was formerly a Buddhistic temple. The idols that we see both in and about the temple prominently suggest Budhistic sculpture. When the religion of Gautama passed from its high meridian glory in India and hastened towards dissolution, this shrine appears to have been converted into a place of Hindu worship. On the image of the 3 Rishis there, we find marks of the holy ashes. But these images are old by thousands of years. There is a pretty legend in connection with this temple. A pious Brahmin Poti had a dutiful wife. One morning he went to bathe and she boiled a small quantity of rice for offering to the deity. In his absence,, three pandarams begged her rice, for meals. Finding nothing, she gave away the rice she boiled for her husband's puja. When the Poti returned and learned this, he got angry and beat her once. She ran on and finding a line of boiled rice lying on the ground before her, she followed that, which ultimately led her to the site of this shrine. Her husband also followed her and reached the same. The three pandarams, they say, represent the Hindu Trinity. The Potis' wife was suddenly metamorphosed into goddess Bhagavati. The Poti is said to stand before his wife saying that he beat her only once. In the temple there is only one Puja a day and five measures of rice are allowed—perhaps one for each. With reference to this temple H. H. the late Maharajah emphatically wrote:—"The Brahmins have appropriated and adapted to their purposes, this Budhistic temple." Thus it was, in the words of Logan, that "Vedic Brahmanism is believed to have finally supplanted Jainism."

He adds:—"In [Malabar proper, the style] for architecture) is reserved almost if not altogether for religious edifices. In Travancore it is often to be seen in lay buildings...How the Mohamedans came to adopt this style for their mosques is to be accounted for by the tradition that some at least of the original mosques were built on the sites of temples."

CHAPTER IV.—MAHOMEDANISM.

The Mahomedans in this country are mostly converts from Hindus. They seldom furnish converts to the Christian faith. They are found in all Taluqs. They number over one and half lacs. They are a strong and hardy race. They are divided into several classes. The chief sub divisions are (1) Sunnis and (2) Shias. The former is again cut up into Hanifee, Shafee, Malikee and Hambali. The latter consists of six groups. Each of these groups is sub-divided into 12 classes. Each of the two main classes regards the other as wanderers from the truth. Mahomedanism is known as the antagonistic creed. The Koran is the sacred scripture of the Mahomedans. Mahomet is their prophet. Their doctrine is there is no god but god and Mahomet is his prophet. They conceive that there are seven hells and seven heavens. As observed by Sir Monier Williams: "The Moslems of India became partially Hinduised, and in language, habits and character, they took from the Hindus more than they imparted. Hence it happens that the lower orders of the Mahomedans observe distinctions of caste as strictly as the Hindus." Many of them will eat and drink together but not intermarry. There are about 500 mosques in Travancore. The priests are called Thangals. There are 54 mosques in Trivandrum. This represents the highest number. Next comes Kalculam, the former capital of the country. Even in the essentially Christian centre of Kottayam, there is one mosque.

The history of Mahomedanism is easily stated. Tradition ascribes its origin to a writ obtained by Shaik-ibn-Dinar and his family from the last Perumal. He and his family set out for Malabar bearing the Perumal's letters. They delivered the letters to whom they were addressed. They obtained ready acceptance and recognition at the hands of his chiefs whose territories they visited with a view to spread and propogate the faith of Islam. The Kodungalor chief was the first prince they visited. They were received hospitably and given lands to build mosques on. Malik-ibn-Dinar became the firt Kazi of the place. He sent to Travancore Kollam (Quilon) Malik-ibn-Habib with his wife and some of their children. The Travancore Maha-Rajah received them hospitably and gave also lands to build mosques on. The second great mosque was founded there by Hussain, one of the sons of Malik-ibn-Habib who became its Kazi. The last of the famous Malabar mosques was constructed at Quilon. All this took place about the first half of the twelth century which was an important era in the history of the Malabar coast.

CHAPTER V.—CHRISTIANITY.

It is an interesting feature that Travancore has a larger Christian population than any other Native state, 20 p.c. of the people of the state being Christians. The proportion of Christians to other population is 29 times that of British India—an unmistakable proof of the wisdom and tolerance of the Maha Rajahs of this state from very early times. The history of Christian Mission in Travancore may be traced under two broad divisions namely, Syrian Mission (comprehending Catholic Mission) and Protestant Mission (including Church Mission and London Mission).

The Syrian Mission. The earliest Christian Mission is ascribed by tradition to the advent of St. Thomas the apostle in the 1st century of the Christian era. It will be seen therefore that the history of Christianity in this country is a history of over 1800 years. St. Thomas worked well. He made numerous converts and built several Churches. But on his death there was a great relaxation. The enthusiasm for the new creed became so much cooled down that after the lapse of two centuries there were only 8 families of Christians. However there arrived in 345 A. D., a large colony of Christians from Bagdad, Nineve, Jerusalam and other places under the guidance of Thomas Cana, a merchant who was then trading in the Malabar Coast. They were largely patronised by the early Kings of

Malabar. With their advent and under their influence, the Syrians increased in number and power. Chaldean Bishops also came from Babylon, off and on. These Bishops governed the Churches until the arrival of the Portuguese in 1498 A. D. When the Portuguese Government grew in power, they began to bring the Syrians under the sway of the Portuguese prelates. In 1581 a college appears to have been opened at Vaipicotta where they settled, to impart instruction in priesthood to the local Syrians. Mr. Mackenzie says in his work on Christianity in Travancore that "in 1583 when Father Alex. Valignano returned from Japan, he found awaiting him his appointment as Provincial of the Jesuits and he at once set to work on the systematic instruction of the Thomas Christians." The Syrian Bishop at this time was Mar Joseph. He was suspected of Nestorian heresy and in consequence was arrested and sent to Portugal and afterwards to Rome where "his piety and erudition had aroused a feeling in his favour." But he died there. In the mean time at the request of the Syrians, the Nestorian patriarch of Babylon sent Mar Abraham appointing him to be the Arch-Bishop of Angamali. He was arrested by the Portuguese and detained in the Dominican convent. But he escaped and came to Babylon where the Patriarch reconferred on him the title of the Bishop of Malabar. He then proceeded to Rome and appealed to the Pope. The Pope confirmed him in his appointment.

Supported thus by the Portuguese authorities as well as the Pope, Mar Abraham came. He held a Synod in 1583 at which he made a profession of the Catholic faith, and the Syrian missal was corrected. The Nestorian patriarch of Babylon questioned the conduct of Mar Abraham whose explanation only aggravated his offence. In 1592 he was excommunicated by the Council of Goa which he refused to attend. In 1595 Pope Clement VIII dispatched to Meneze, the Archbishop of Goa, a brief to enquire into the faith of Mar Abraham and of his followers. The synod of Diamper was held in 1599 at which the faith of the Syrians was enunciated. The union of the churches continued from 1596-1653 when it was dissolved. This was hastened by the fall of the Portuguese power in India. When the power of the Portuguese fell, the papal power was disowned. A division took place among the Syrians. Some rejected the power of the Portuguese prelates and declared themselves independent. They formed a new sect, hence known as Puthen Kuttukars, while those who remained steadfast to Rome were called Pazayakuttukars and they continued to remain under the European ecclesiasts. The seceded syrians wrote to several patriarchs in Asia to send a rightly consecrated Syrian Bishop. A Jacobite Bishop, Gregory, came and reconsecrated Mar Thomas I and henceforth a long succession of native matrons governed the Puthencoor Syrians. With the commencement of the

Dutch power in India, new dissensions arose. But as remarked by Mr. Mackenzie in his exhaustive and excellent work on Christianity in Travancore, " they seemed to have concerned themselves little about the Christians except from political reasons." The year 1806 is rendered memorable by the visit of Dr. Cladius Buchanan. He saw Colonel Macaulay, the British Resident in Travancore, and with him visited the Northern parts of the country. At Ankamale, he was presented with a copy of the old Syriac Bible which was in the possession of the Syrians for over 1000 years. It was taken to England and published there. The year 1816 opened a fresh chapter. It begins with the consecration of Mar Dionysius III. Col. Munro was the Resident at the time. He undertook to get out missionaries from Europe. The Church Mission entered into friendly relation with the Syrians. Of the Church Mission itself, we shall speak later on. This relation did not last long. The last portion of the history of the Syrian church discloses how under Mar Dionysius IV it severed its connection with the Anglican missionaries ; how a special commission sat to adjudicate the claims on the endowments of the Kottayam seminary ; how both the parties languished under 10 years of litigation and how in the end Mar Dionysius obtained a decree in his favour. Mar Dionysius the head of the non-reforming partyand Mar Thoma the head of the reforming party have between them the whole of the Travancore Churches.

We have already remarked that the Church Mission owed its existence to Col. Munro. He undertook to get out missionaries to train Syrian deacons to carry on parochial schools. Thomas Norton arrived in 1816, and he was followed by Mr. Bailey, in November of that year. Then came Messrs Baker and Fenn. Mr. Fenn was put in charge of the Seminary. H. H's. Government endowed the institution with 20,000 Rs. and a large estate at Kallada called, "Munro Island". More than this, the tolerant and liberal Government of His Highness helped Mr. Bailey in the translation and distribution of the Bible, with another gift of Rs. 8,000. Col. Munro got the Honourable East India Company to invest 3,000 Star pagodas in the name of the community for educational purposes. Col. Munro was the most earnest promoter of the Syrian Christian interests. There is an illustrious roll of Missionaries who have laboured in this mission. It has several remarkable educational institutions and its principal station is Kottayam.

London Mission:—This owed its early beginnings to the enthusiastic efforts of its first convert Veda Manikam. At his instance, Rev. Tobias Willam Ringletaube came from Tranquebar in 1806, and built at Myladia Church in 1809 with the courteous consent of H. H. Lekshmi Rani. The construction of the Church was commanded to be su pervised, by Tahsildar Munnen Annavi. The benevolent Rani endowed the Church with 100 cotas of of paddy land, of which the revenue is now devoted to the support of the Nagercoil Mission College. Rev. Ringletaube was succeeded by Mr. Mead who came in 1816. H. H. the Rani was pleased to place at his disposal a Sircar building with extensive premises and to make a grant of Rs, 5,000 to enable him to buy more lands for Mission purpose. The tax on the paddy lands was also reduced. These concessions are in keeping with the tolerance and magnanimity characteristic of the Royal House of Travancore, so evident from the following pregnant utterance of H. H. the Maharajah :—"The aid given to the Schools and other institutions established by the good missionaries who labour so disinterestedly is no more than the assistance they have a right to expect, who help us so materially in promoting the intellectual and moral advancement of our people." Mr. Mead was joined by Mr. Knill, and other missionaries. In 1819 Mr. Knill laid the foundation of the Nagercoil chapel. The London mission Society has stations at (1) Nagercoil where Mission work began in 1818. (2) Neyyor where Mission work commenced in 1827 (3) Parasala where Mission work was started in 1845. (4) Trivandrum where it was set on foot in 1837 and (5) Quilon where it was organized in 1821. It is now 96 years since the work of Christian mission was started in South Travancore and under Rev. Mr. Duthie the present energetic and enthusisastic leader of it, the mission has progressed and prospered considerably.

These are some of the several religious creeds and social castes in this ancient land of an ancient people. Lord Curzon is perfectly right when he observes:—"In one respect His Highness enjoys a peculiar position of responsibility, for he is the Ruler of a community that is stamped by wide racial differences and represents a curious motley of religions." The continuous prevalence of peace among them is an unerring proof of the fact that the Maharajah has "no higher ambition than to show consideration to the low and equity and tolerance to all."

Progress.

CHAPTER I.—A HISTORICAL RETROSPECT.

Travancore and its Royal House are of very ancient existence. Both are mentioned in the edicts of Asoka. Recent epigraphical and archaeological researches show that the kingdom of Travancore embraced a considerably larger area of territory than is included within its present boundaries. There is no doubt that the Travancore Royal Family is the modern representative of the Chera dynasty which exercised sovereignty from very early times. In the report on Epigraphy for the last year embodied in the Madras G. O. No. 855 dated 22nd August, it is said that in his letter Francis Xavier, the Portuguese missionary, mentions the great king of Travancore and speaks of him as "having authority over all south India" It is also said that "early in the 14th century, a king of Travancore appears to have made the Pandiyas and the Cholas subject to the Keralas". But in the wars that followed, Travancore lost its possession beyond the ghauts. Like Kolathunaud, Yerunaud and Perumpadappu, it formed one of the four principalities into which Kerala or ancient Malabar was divided. These principalities owned at first the supremacy of the Chera kings. The first Cheraman Perumal was installed in 344 A. D. The period of the Perumals came to a close with the disappearance of the last of them. Some writers think that he was expelled by popular revolt Others are of opinion that he went away to embrace a new religion—some say the faith of Islam and others, Christianity. There is another class yet who believe that he became a Budhist. Be this what it may, his disappearance was the immediate signal for the local Rajahs to assume leadership. Accordingly, the Kolath Swarupam of the Kolathnaud Rajah, the Nidiyirip Swarupam of the Yernaud Raja, the Perumpadappu Swarupam of the Cochin Rajah, and the Tripapur Swarupam of the Travancore Rajah asserted their independence. These events took place in the 9th century.

In 824 A. D. Udaya Marthanda Varma founded the Kollam era now obtaining in Malabar. There are two well-known places called Kollam. One is in North Malabar : the other in Travancore. The Northern Kollam era commences on 1st Kanni (September). The Southern Kollam era commences on 1st Chingam, the Jodiac month of Leo. There are several theories set up to account for this difference. The founding of Kollam, the acquisition of independance by the Kolathiri Rajas (North and South) and the advent of Sankaracharayar, are some of the important events associated with the theories. However that be, Mr. Logan asserts that the two historical events from which the era is supposed to begin, are the institution of the great national festival of Onam and the disappearance of the last Perumal. The first precisely falls about the same time. There is ample evidence to prove the latter.

(1) At Cranganore, the people keep ready wooden shoes and water in expectation of the Perumal's return.

(2) The Maharajas of Travancore on receiving the coronation sword have still to declare "I will keep the sword until the return of my uncle".

(3) The Zamorins too at their coronation have still, when crossing the Kallayi ferry, to take betel from the hands of a man dressed up as a Mapilla woman.

The king of Travancore in whose time the new era was founded died in 830 A. D. Little is known of the history of the kingdom for the next five centuries. About 1330 A. D. Aditya Varma was king. He was succeeded in 1335 by Veeramartnanda Varma who reigned prosperously for 40 years. The next king was Chera Udaya Marthanda Varma whose reign lasted for 62 years. He ruled over all the south east possessions of Travancore and Tinnevelly side. There is an inscription of this king at Cheranmahadevi in the Tinnevelly District, dated 1439. He was succeeded by Venattu Mutharajah. From this date till the latter part of the 17th century, there is no account of the reign of Travancore Sovereigns, but merely a list of names.

In 1677 the numerous feaudatory chiefs flew into open rebellion against the ruling power. Aditya Varma the reigning King was poisoned and five Princes of the reigning family were murdered. Umayamma Ranee then became Regent the only surviving Prince being a Minor. She called to her aid one of her relations Kerala Varma to put down the rising. She handed over to him the sole administration and it is from that date that the accurate history of the province can be continuously traced.

In 1680 a Mahomedan adventurer established himself at the capital. He was however defeated and killed by the Regent's General Kerala Varma. In 1684 the young Prince Ravi Varma attained majority and ascended the throne. He was succeeded in 1718 by Unni Kerala Varma. The next king was Rama Varma who entered into an alliance treaty with the King of Madura in 1726. In 1729 Rama Varma was succeeded by Marthanda Varma. He found the country in a very unsettled condition. He faced the difficulties bravely and over-came them successfully. He secured the country from foreign aggression by constructing a wall at the southern frontier from Kadukari to the Cape, and new forts, bastions, batteries and powder Magazines. He quelled the rebellion of the local barons who rose in a body against the king. He repaired and reconstructed the national state shrine at Trivandrum. He undertook gigantic irrigation works in Nanjanad. Having restored peace and order, he extended the limits of the kingdom. In the course of fifteen years, he extended the country from Edavai to the Periyar. In the words of Sir Madava

Row, this king "was one of the most remarkable figures in the history of Travancore. The most remarkable feature of his reign was the uniform and unvarying good fortune that attended him in all his enterprise for the benefit of the country." He died in 1758 and was succeeded by Bala Rama Varma who has since been known as Rāma Varma the Great.

Under Rama Varma the Great:—His reign extended from 1758-1779. He enlarged and improved the army and put down the remaining barons who had raised their heads against the central authority. Haider Ali, the commander of a detachment of the Mysore Army dethroned its Hindu monarch and usurped the throne in 1751. Vanchi Bala Rama Varma granted a free passage to the British troops marching against the French partisans of Haidar at Mahe in the year 1772. He also manfully resisted the temptations held out to him by Tippu, son of Haider, to espouse his cause against the English with whom he was waging a deadly war. In 1784 the Rajah of Travancore lent his support to the British troops and it was mainly through his assistance that Tippu was defeated in the engagement. The British Government in recognition of the signal services thus rendered by the Rajah included him as a steadfast ally in the treaty of 1784 between the East India Company and the Sultan of Mysore In their letter to the Maharajah, the Commissioners say: "The Company did not on this occasion forget your fidelity and the steady friendship and attachment you have uniformly shewn them in every situation and under every change of fortune. You are expressly named and included in the treaty as their friend and ally: as such we can assure you on the part of the Company that your interest and welfare will always be considered as protected as their own." Tippu Sultan conquered the Districts of Malabar and Canara and next directed his attention to Travancore. The English at the head of a large and well-disciplined army offered him a strong resistance which completely frustrated his scheme He however conquered all the territ ories lying on the borders of Travancore and threatened the Rajah with an invasion. The Rajah applied in 1798 to the British Government to lend him the services of a few English officers to train and discipline his troops. This led to the agreement of 1798 between the Madras Government and the Rajah of Travancore by which the latter secured a subsidiary force of two battalions of the Company's army to be stationed on his frontiers at a cost of 1775 pagodas (about Rs. 6500) a month to be paid in cash or in pepper. Tippu made preparations to march on to Travancore and to completly overthrow the Hindu rule. The Travancore Rajah had recently purchased from the Dutch Government two fortresses built by them on the northern outskirts of Travancore. He had further constructed round them a strong wall 30 miles long on the borders of Mysore and Travancore extending from the Anamalai Hills to the sea. Tippu at the head of a large army encamped in the neighbourhood of this wall in December 1789 and attempted to storm these fortresses. But the English in return for the past service of their faithful ally sent a large army to the Rajah's support under the command of General Meadows. When he heard that the English Army was hastening to the succour of the Rajah, he returned to Serrangapatam and raised a large army to oppose the arms of the English. The English first opened campaigns by reducing the strongholds of Tippu near Coimbatore. Tippu marched against them but was defeated and repulsed. The portion of Travancore conquered by Tippu was soon recovered and restored to the Rajah. The Raja died in 1798. Of him Fra. Bartalomeo says: " For my part I could not help admiring the goodness of heart, affability and humanity of this prince as well as the simplicity of his household establishment and way of life". He adds that during his reign " public security is restored throughout the country; robbery and murder are no longer heard of; no one has occasion to be afraid on the highways; religious work is never interrupted; the people may rest assured that on every occasion, justice will be speedily administered. An English man seldom prone to indulge in the language of adulation called the Raja the father of the people". The English Commissioners who sat on the Malabar land settlement of 1792 have put on record:—"We own, he left a favourable impression on our minds both as to the personal good qualities and what we consider as unequivocal sincerity of his attachment to the East India Company".

This Raja was succeeded by his nephew also called Rama Varma. During the reign of this Raja, the office of the Resident was first instituted by the East India Company and the first to hold that office was Col. Macaulay who arrived in Travancore in 1800. The Raja entered into a fresh treaty with the British power in 1805. This treaty confirmed the sincere and cordial relations of peace and amity between the Raja and the East India Company. It is known as the Treaty of perpetual friendship and alliance between them. By this treaty the Rajah was required to pay for a native regiment in addition to the subsidy fixed in 1795 (in all 8 lacs of Rs. a year) and further to share the expenses of his large forces when necessary; to pay at all times the utmost attention to the advice of the British Government; to hold no communication with any foreign state; and to admit no European foreigners into his service or to allow him to remain in his territory without the sanction of the British Government. Raja Rama Varma died in 1811.

Under Regency of Ranis:—His sister Lakshmi Ranee occupied the throne till she was delivered of a son. With the aid and advice of Colonel Munro who acted also as Dewan, she managed the affairs of the country with much prudence and courage. Under them the old laws which assigned higher punishments to minor offences and lighter to those of a graver kind were modified in keeping with the advancing age and new laws promulgated whereby punishment varied with the gravity of the offence. Justice began to be equitably administered both to the rich and the poor like. In the words of the Madras Manual of administration "Tranquility was restored : the public service was reorganised : debts discharged and the financial prosperity of the kingdom secured". After a brief reign of 3 years, Lakshmi Ranee died leaving two sons and a daughter, all in infancy.

She was succeeded by Parvathi Ranee who though only 13 years of age, ruled as Regent during the minority of the late Ranee's eldest son. She governed the country with marked ability for 15 years. During her reign various missionary agencies were permitted to settle in the country and were generously encouraged by donations in money and land from the Ranee. Col. Munro in his report to the Madras Government says :—" The temporal situation of the Syrians has also been naturally improved. I have frequently taken occasion to bring to the notice of Her Highness the Ranee of Travancore, and her intelligent, liberal and ingenuous mind has also appeared to feel a deep interest in their history, misfortunes and character. She is aware of the attention excited to their situation in Europe and their anxiety to manifest a sincerity of her attachment to the British nation has formed, I believe, an additional motive for the kindness and generosity she has uniformly displayed towards the Syrians. She has appointed a considerable number of them to public Offices and lately presented the sum of Rs. 20,000 to the College of Kottayam as an endowment for its support. The Syrians are most grateful for her goodness and cherish in no ordinary degree the sentiments of affection and respect towards her person, that are entertained by every class of her subjects."

It was during her reign that the Nair Brigade was organised. Captain Macton was its first Commandant. During her reign, exaction of Inam or free service from the Christians was prohibited. Stamped Cadjan documents were introduced: restrictions against the wearing of golden jewels by Nair women were removed and cultivation of coffee and other industrial pursuits were encouraged,

Under the later Rajas:—In 1829 Prince Rama Varma ascended the Musnad. He was an able ruler. He did much for the improvement of his subjects. He abolished many grievous taxes. He laid the foundation of the modern system of education by establishing an English School at Trivandrum in 1840. He also erected an Observatory and took a most intelligent interest in science and other branches of learning. The removal of the Huzur Cutcherry and other institutions from

Quilon to Trivandrum ; the improvement of the Nair Brigade: the abolition of the Huzur Courts for the first time: the promulgation of a new Law Code on the model of the British establishment; the commencement of Survey operations and the introduction of printing and lithography are some of the important measures during his reign. He was a great scholar and linguist. He had extraordinary talents and fine taste for the fine arts which he much encouraged. He was a great poet and composed verses in Sanskrit, Malayalam, Telugu and Marathi. Mr. Brown says:—"His Highness was celebrated throughout India for his love of learning, for a cultivated mind, great poetical powers, knowledge of many languages. His Highness is well-known also for his decision of character. In his latter years, his health became much impaired and he devoted much time and money to religious and charitable purposes. He died in 1845.

His brother Marthanda Varma succeeded him He was a well educated and enlightened ruler. He collected and contributed articles for the London Exhibition of 1857. He regulated the admission of pauper suits. He imported Bengal rice to meet the scarcity caused by the great flood. He abolished slavery by Royal Proclamation. He settled the right of Christian converts to move among and to assume the costume of the higher classes. He did away with the monopoly of pepper. He revised the tariff Value of articles and gave facility for increased trade. It was during his reign that Sir Madava Row was appointed Dewan and Lord Harris, Governor of Madras visited Travancore. The Eastern Fort gate was constructed. He opened the "Victoria Anantha Marthanda Canal" for the benefit of cultivation in South Travancore. He attained much skill in medicine. He reigned for 14 years and died in 1860. Mr. Brown records:—"His Highness was a warm-breasted gentleman whose death was regretted by all who knew him. His knowledge of science, though greatest in Chemistry, gave him a personal interest in the Observatory, and he was prepared to accept any proposition likely to aid the work done in it. I shall never cease to entertain with liveliest feelings His Highness' memory"

Under the Maharajas:—He was succeeded by his nephew Rama Varma who inaugurated a brilliant epoch in the history of Travancore. Gifted with talents of a high order, he pursued a most liberal and enlightened policy. He reformed the administrative and executive machinery of the state. Law Courts were organised. Magisterial powers were conferred on division officers. Heavy import duties were abolished. Excise rates were reduced. Hereditary robbers were put down and expelled. Public buildings were reared. Bridges, Canals and tunnels were constructed. Forests were reclaimed; waste lands were cultivated and new industries encouraged. In recognition of his excellent administraion a Sannad was conferred upon him by the Paramount power direct- that he should be addressed by the title of ***Maha-Rajah*** in all communications from the British Government. He was created a Knight Grand Commander of the most exalted order of the Star of India, and a Councillor of the Indian Empire. He gained for the country the apellation of the "Model State" which it still retains. After 20 years of progressive activity, he died in 1880.

He was succeeded by his brother Rama Varma. He was a brilliant Scholar in English and Sanskrit and a particular patron and promoter of education, progress and enlightenment During his short but most brilliant reign, the administrative machinery was mostly recast and remodelled on an improved system and the period was marked by the introduction of a long series of progressive measures. He introduced important reforms in the Revenue, Judicial, Educational, Police, Medical, and Municipal departments of the state and opened several works of public utility. His subjects enjoyed plenty and prosperity during his reign. He died at the age of 48 in 1885. In 1882 he was invested with the Knight Grand Commandership of the most exalted order of the Star of India, and almost all the scientific institutions of Europe showered honours on him. He was a Fellow of the Linnian Society, London: of the Royal Geographical society: of the Royal Asiatic society of

Great Britain and Ireland: of the Statistical society of London; of the *Society de ettute colonial a maritime* Paris. He was also admitted by the French Government to the order of "*Officer De La Instruction Publique.*" In fact, as observed by that acute observer of human intelligence and character, Sir. M. E. Grant Duff, this ruler "was the typical example of the influence of English thought upon the south Indian mind."

He is succeeded by H. H. the Maharaja who ascended the musnud in 1885. Since his accession, the country has progressed by giant strides. The existence of four arts colleges; the establishment of training schools to teach the principles and practice of teaching; of agricultural schools to impart instruction in elementary theoretical and practical agriculture: of the Industrial School of Arts where a systematic course of instruction is given in drawing, designs, and painting; of a Sanskrit college to represent the Oriental faculty; of medical schools to train Hospital Assistants; of a Survey school to teach surveying to the Revenue and Judicial subordinates; of educationsl boards in view to enlist the sympathy and co-operation of men of local influence and public spirit; and of a scheme of public lectures answering to the university extension scheme, prove beyond doubt that every facility which the practical sagacity of a ruler can suggest, is afforded for intellectual development. Again, by the granting of agricultural loans: by the holding of agricultural exhibition; by the organisation of an agricultural demonstration farm and school; by the remission of several obnoxious taxes which pressed heavily on industry; by the Settlement of the longstanding dispute between land-lords and tenants; and by comprehensive land survey and assessment, the interests of the rural population have been considerably advanced. Besides these, several public works, designed for the protection and promotion of agriculture, such as the Kodayar Irrigation project; the Parur and Kaipuzhai reclamation schemes; the Kynagari and Puthencara bunds; the restoration of the banks of several rivers; the construction of bridges and anicuts across innumerable rivers and streams, have also been carried out. Similarly the installation of gas-light; the introduction of the Railway; and the construction of the High Range road are other measures calculated to expand industry. Then again, the organisation of a Sanitary Department including Vaccination, vital statistics, rural sanitation and itinerant medical relief, and the contribution of medical grants to Hospitals, Dispensaries and Native Vaidyasalas demonstrate how largely the health of the people is promoted. And above all, the establishment of the Legislative Council marks the inauguration of an important era. Every administrative measure of His Highness' reign is inspired by a genuine solicitude for the welfare of the people. We propose in the following pages to concentrate on the main lines of progress, the scattered rays which it furnishes.

CHAPTER II.—POLITICAL RELATIONS.

The present political relation of the state with the Paramount Power is governed by the Treaty of 1805. The articles of that treaty are therefore reproduced below:

1. The friends and enemies of either of the contracting parties shall be considered as the friends and enemies of both. The Honourable the East India Company Behauder especially engaging to defend and protect the territories of the Maharajah Ram Rajah Behauder of Travancore against all enemies whatever.

2. Whereas by the seventh article of the treaty concluded in the year 1795 between the Maharajah Ram Rajah Behauder and the English East India Company Behaudur, it was stipulated, " that when the Company shall require any aid of his troops to assist them in war it shall be incumbent on the said reigning Rajah, for the time being to furnish such aid, to such extent and in such numbers as may be in his power, from his regular infantry and cavalry. exclusive of the native Nayars of the country" and the Company being now willing entirely to release the Rajah from the obligations incurred under the said stipulation, it is hereby concluded and agreed, that Ram Rajah Behauder is for ever discharged from the aforesaid burthensome obligation.

3. In consideration of the stipulation and release contained in the first and second articles, whereby the Company become liable to heavy and constant expense, while great relief is afforded to the revenues of the Rajah, His Highness engages to pay annually to the said Company a sum equivalent to the expense of one regiment of the honourable Company's native infantry, in addition to the sum now payable by the said Rajah for the force subsidised by His Highness, by the 3rd article of the Subsidiary treaty of 1795, the said amount to be paid in six equal instalments commencing from the first day of January 1805 and His Highness further agrees that the disposal of the sum together with the arrangement and employment of the troops to be maintained by it, whether stationed within the Travancore country or within the Company's Districts, shall be left entirely to the Company.

4. Should it become necessary for the Company to employ force more than that which is stipulated for in the preceding article, to protect the territories of the said Maharajah against attack or invasion, His Highness agrees to contribute, jointly with the Company towards the discharge of the increaseed expense thereby occasioned, such a sum as shall appear on an attentive consideration of His said Highness to bear a just and reasonable proportion to the actual net revenues of His said Highness.

5. Whereas it is indispensably necessary that effecutal and lasting security should be provided against any failure in the funds destined to defray either the expenses of the permanent military force in time of peace, or the extraordinary expenses described in the preceding articles of the present treaty, it is hereby stipulated and agreed between the contracting parties, that whenever the Governor-General-in-Council of Fort William in Bengal, shall have reason to apprehend such failure in the funds so destined, the said Governor-General in Council shall be at liberty and shall have full power and right either to introduce such regulations and ordinances as he shall deem expedient for the internal management and collection of the Revenues or for the better ordering of any other branch and department of the Government of Travancore, or to assume and bring under the direct management of the servants of the said company Behauder such part or parts of the territorial possessions of His Highness The Mah Rajah Rama Rajah Behauder as shall appear to him, the said Governor-General in Council, necessary to render the funds efficient and available, either in time of peace or war.

6. And it is hereby further agreed, that when ever the said Governor-General in Council shall signify to the said Maha Rajah Rama Rajah Behauder that it is become necessary to carry into effect the provisions of the fifth article, His said Highness Maha Rajah Rama Rajah Behauder shall

immediately issue orders to his aumils or other officers either for carrying into effect the said regulation andordinances, according to the fifth article or placing the territories acquired under the exclusive authority and control of the English company Behauder, and in case His Highness shall not issue orders within ten days from the time when the application shall have been formally made to him, then the said Governor-General in Council shall be at liberty to issue orders, by his own authorities, either for carrying into effect the said regulation and ordinances, or for assuming the management and collection of the Revenues of the said territorties as he shall Judge expedient for the purpose of securing the efficiency of the said military funds and of providing for the effectual protection of the country and welfare of the people. Provided always that whenever and so long as any part or parts of His said Highness' territories shall be placed and shall remain under the exclusive authority and control of the said East India Company, the Governor-General in Council shall render to His Excellency a true and faithful account of the revenue and produce of the territories so assumed. Provided also that in case whenever His Highness' actual receipt or annual income, arising from the territorial revenues be less than the sum of 2 lacs of Rupees together with one fifth of the net revenues of the whole of his territories which sum of two lacs cf Rupees together with one fifth of the net revenue of the whole of the territories which sum of 1/5 of the said revenues the East India company engages, at all times and in every possible case to secure and cause to be paid for Highness' use.

7. His Highness the Maha Rajah Ram Rajah Behauder engages that he will be guided by a sincere and cordial attention to the relation of peace and amity established between the English company and their allies and that he will carefully abstain from any interference in the affairs of any state in alliance with the said English Company Behauder or of any state whatever. And for securing the object of this stipulation, it is further stipulated and agreed that no communication or correspondence with any foreign state whatever, shall be holden by His said Highness without the previous knowledge and sanction of the said English Company Behauder.

8. His Highness stipulates and agrees that he will not admit any European foreigners into his service without the concurrence of the English Company Behaudur, and that he will apprehend and deliver to the Companys' Government all Europeans of whatever description who shall be found within the territories of His said Highness without regular passports from the British Government, it being His Highness' determined resolution not to suffer even for a day any European to remain within his territories unless by consent of the said Company

9. Such parts of the Treaty (A. D. 1795) one thousand seven hundred and ninety five between the English East India Company and the late Rajah of Travancore as are calculated to strengthen the alliance, to cement the friendship and to identify the interest of the contracting parties, are hereby renewed and confirmed; and accordingly His Highness hereby promises to pay, at all times, utmost attention to such advice as the English Government shall occasionally judge it necessary to offer him with a view to the economy of his finances, the better collection of his revenues, the administration of justice, the extension of commerce, the encouragement of trade, agriculture and industry or any other objects connected with the advancement of His Highness' interests, the happiness of his people and the mutual welfare of both states.

10. This treaty consisting of 10 articles, being this day the 14th day of January 1805 settled and concluded at the fortress of Teeroovanamapuram in Travancore, by Lieutenant Colonel Colin Macaulay, on behalf and in the name of His Excellency the Most Noble Marquis Wellesley, Governor-General in Council with the Maha Rajah Ram Rajah Behauder, he has delivered to the said Maha Rajah one copy of the same in English and Persian, signed and sealed by him and His Highness the Maha Raja has delivered to the Lieutenant Colonel aforesaid, another copy also in Persian and English bearing his seal and signature and signed and sealed by Valoo Tumpy, Dewan to the Maha Raja

aforesaid; and the Lieutenant Colonel aforesaid has engaged to procure and deliver to the said Maha rajah without delay, a copy of the same, under the seal and signature of His Excellency the Most Noble Marquis of Wellesley, Governor-General in council, on the receipt of which by the said Maha Rajah, the present treaty shall be deemed complete and binding on the Honorable Company and on the Maha Rajah Ram Rajah Behauder, and the copy of it now delivered to the said Maha Rajah shall be returned.

The Nair Brigade.—It is a remnant of the army of Travancore which was disbanded after the insurruction of 1808. Col Munro proposed to the Madras Government at the instance of the Travancore Ranee that the strength of this force be increased and commanded by a European officer. In 1819 the proposal was sanctioned and the present Nair Brigade was initiated. The first officer to hold command was Captain Gray. The term Nair Brigade came to be used only from and after 1830, In 1838, the force was armed with flint fuzils. In 1871, a scale of pension was fixed for the Brigade Sepoys and in 1875 it was revised and three years later a higher scale of pay was given them. Since its organisation 20 European officers have commanded the force. The duties of the force consist "in guarding forts, palaces, treasuries, jails, pagodas, stores, and Cutcherries; in assisting civil officers, in repressing riots or tumults; and in furnishing escorts for the members of the Royal family and on public state occasions." The Body guard establishment consists of 60 horses and 40 privates. They have also the necessary complement of officers. Recently a new battalion styled the first battalion is organized. The recruits thereof are required to live in Government lines. They will be liable to serve in any part of the state. They are eligible for pension after 21 years' service.

Adoption:—Of the several political events that have happened during the period under notice, none will be comparable in importance to the adoptions made in the Royal House. During the reign of Umayamma Rani it was felt necessary to perpetuate the Royal line by a fresh adoption. All her sons with only one exception having been foully murdered, and the Rani having been surrounded by disloyal and treacherous persons, she felt also the need of external support. In those days, Cherakkal was a more opulant Kingdom than Travancore. She accordingly applied to the Cherakkal Rajah to strengthen their ties by letting two girls from his family to be adopted by her. But as the Rajah had held in great contempt and hated his Southern relative, he played a practical joke upon the Rani by sending two Pandalai girls. The Rani discovered this and did not know what to do. Just then a Koil Tampuran of the Thattari Koilagam happened to visit her court on his return from Ramaswaram. To him the helpless Rani applied for aid. He sympathised with her and promised to bring two of his daughters belonging to the Junior Branch of the Kolathnad family.

True to his word he brought two princes who were duly adopted in 856. M E. and shortly afterwards married to his own nephews. One of them died; but the other gave birth to the great Marthanda Varma Rajah to whom the country owes its present territorial extent. It was only after the grant of the Kilimanur estate in 903 M. E. to the members of the Koil Tampuran's family in recognition of the meritorious services rendered by the Koil Tampuran, the Thattari Koilagom family finally established itself in Travancore. From the time of Raja Marthanda Varma down to the regency of Parvathi Rani, all the sovereigns of Travancore were descended from the Koil Tampurans of Kilimanur. The other families of Koil Tampurans entered Travancore as refugees during the invasion of Malabar by the Mysore Tyrants and the famou Rama Rajah who reigned in Travancore at that time, most magnanimously received them into his protection. The families of Koil Tampurans settled at present in Travancore are :—Thattari Koilagom, (Kilimanur); Pazanchery Koilagom (including the families of Changanacherry, Anantapuram); Chembramadom Koilagom: (Tiruvellah, Pallam, and Grammam): Cherical Koilagom (Mavelikara); Panangad Koilagom (Chengannur). Rani Lekshmi Bhai, who was connected with the Kilimanur house through her father was the first to marry into the Changancherry family. The late lamented Senior Rani also chose her consort from the same family Her consort, Kerala Varma Valia Koil Tampuran, is an ornament alike to the family he represents and to the literature of the country in promoting which he devotes his best talents and energies. Unfortunately there is no offspring by this union. Her late Highness the Junior Rani on the other hand, mingled her heart in conjugal felicity with a member of of the Kilimanur house, the late Kochu Koil Tampuran. He died in the prime of life in 1048 M. E. a year after the birth of H. H. the late first Prince, the youngest of his four sons, who in the words of Lord Curzon "seemed destined to cast a fresh lustre on the name of the famous ancester which he bore." It is terrible that all the four sons, heirs to the throne, died a premature death—a severe calamity unprecedented in the history of Travancore. It is however satisfactory to note that in perpetuation of the Royal line, Their Highnesses the present Senior and Junior Ranis, both of the Mavelikarai family, have with the concurrence of the British Government been adopted on the 31st August 1900. By this adoption the direct relationship with the Kilimanur nobility is fast maintained. The Ranis are the grand daughters of the celebrated Indian Artist Mr. Ravi Varma Koil Tampuran whose name stands on fame's lofty pinnacle raised by the spontaneous homage of the enlightened æsthetic world. Lord Curzon has eloquently echoed the wishes of the people when he expressed the hope that "in due time the expectation raised by this interesting event may meet with fulfilment and that there may never be wanting in the Travancore state a succession of Princes royally born, well nurtured and qualified by instinct and training to carry on its old and honorable traditions." It may be stated here that these adoptions were made in pursuance of the right conferred by Lord Canning's Sannad of March 1862 which runs as follows :—

"Her Majesty being desirous that the Governments of the several Princes and Chiefs of India who now govern their own territories should be perpetuated and that the representation and dignity of their houses should be continued, I hereby, in fulfilment of their desire, convey to you the assurance that on failure of natural heirs, the adoption by yourself and future rulers of your state of a successor according to the Hindu law and to the customs of your race will be recognised and confirmed. Be assured that nothing shall disturb the engagement thus made to you so long as your house is loyal to the crown and faithful to the conditions of the treaties, grants or engagements which record its obligations to the British Government."

The Title of Maharajah :—This has been already referred to. It was conferred on the rulers of this state on 6th August 1866. The following was the notification issued by Sir John Lawrence: "In recognition of your Highness' excellent administration of the Travancore state, I have directed that your Highness shall be addressed by the title of Maharajah in all communications from the British Government." The progressive vigour and efficiency of the administration since then amply justify the retention of the title by successive rulers of this state.

Among other events of political significance may be mentioned the arrangements made as to the jurisdiction over European British subjects and the adoption of a customs convention. These will be dealt with in their proper places. Besides these, there are again the granting of the dignity of a Knight Grand Commander to all the Maharajahs (including the present ruler); the appointment of the Penultimate Maharajah as the Councillor of the Indian Empire; the Imperial assemblage at Delhi; the visits of successive Governors of the Madras Presidency and, for the first time, of H. E. the present Viceroy Lord Curzon; the Golden and Diamond-Jubilee celebrations of Her Majesty the late Queen-Empress Victoria; Royal tours; and last not least, the addition to His Highness the present Maharajah's salute, "signifying in the most conspicuous manner the recognition by the Government of India of his statesmanship and services."

CHAPTER III.—MATERIAL DEVELOPMENT.

Administration,—The Government of the country is conducted in the name and under the control and guidance of H. H. the Maharajah with the advice of the British Resident. The chief minister is called Dewan with whom the British Resident and the local heads of Departments correspond in all official matters. The several Departments of the State are constituted on the British model and the duties, powers and responsibilities of the officers controlling them are clearly laid down under Royal commands. The actual share of the administration which falls to the sovereign is considerable. Sir Seshia Sastri has truly said: "Few have better means of judging of the actual share of the work of the administration which falls to the sovereign and it is nothing but a statement of the bare fact that that share has been greater and far more anxious and heavy than mine" The Maha Raja devotes several hours every day for the disposal of heavy files of papers submitted to him for orders. The personal interest taken by the sovereign in all matters affecting the welfare of the people and his intimate acquaintance with the details of administration are remarkable and commended time and again by the Government of Madras.

For purposes of administration the Country is divided into four Divisions and each Division is presided over by an officer called the Dewan

Peishcar. Till 1856 the Dewan Peishcars were doing duty in the Dewan's office. It was towards the early part of 1856 that Dewan Peishcars were sent out to take charge of the divisions assigned to them.

The history of the Revenue Administration of Travancore is shrouded in obscurity. It is by no means easy to find out from what primordial elements the present system was evolved. What can be gathered from public records of the State is meagre and vague. We find that the credit of having organised for the first time an administrative machinery is due to the genius of Ramien Dalawa. We are inclined to think that the constitution of Dalawa Ramien did not go further than settling the assessment of a large portion of cultivated lands and pointing out some items of expenditure mostly of a religious character to be covered by the increased revenue. The pompous and costly ceremonies, the unnecessary maintenance of a large standing Army ever clamouring for pay and the repeated and heavy demands from the British Government made a strict adherence to the constitution impossible. The successors of Ramien innocently dreaming of a Padmagarbham or to maintain their position were forced to swerve from the rules of the established constitution. Money had to be found somehow. All the engines of authority and power were set in motion. New taxes were imposed on those who offered the least resistance. A large body of illdisciplined army was moving throughout the state to enforce obedience in those who stood up against the extra cesses The most barbarous system of extortion was ruthlessly perpetrated by the treacherous Numburi Dewan who is said to have poisoned Raja Kesava Das. The result was a general rising and revolt of the people at which the heroic bravery of Veloo Tampy, the Hampden of Travancore, prominently displayed itself. This long period of trouble dashed to pieces the machinery of the Revenue administration. This state of affairs soon came to an end About 1012 an attempt seems to have been made to rescue the administration of the land from the province of conflicting customs. In this settlement though a certain degree of fixity and systematic procedure was attained, the chief causes of the disintegration were left untouched. The circulars and rules published from time to time serve only as so many mile-stones in the wearisome search for the vicissitudes that have come upon the settlement of 1012 during the last ten decades and more. After 65 years of unbroken peace, a feeling of national political independence has come into being and the conditions of Revenue administration have in the meanwhile baffled a glorious succession of able Dewans in casting the heterogeneous elements into a consistent and compact body of Revenue rules and regulations. The huge body of these rules and regulations forms the present system of Revenue administration. These rules have been carefully collected and compiled by a native officer in a handsome Manual which is a very useful publication and reflects great credit on the compiler.

It is not our purpose here to enter into the system of land tenures in Travancore. Suffice it to say that there are sixty varieties of Sirkar lands alone which represent their peculiarly complicate nature. Several important measures have been adopted in connection with the administration of land revenue

Survey and Settlement.—As Travancore is an agricultural country, the land forms the main source of revenue. The gathering of land-tax has thus come to be a chief function of the administration. The revenue settlement deals with the principles on which and the process by which such tax is fixed and levied. Its function is threefold. It consists in the accurate measurement of the land, in the ascertainment of its agricultural capacity and in the determination of individual or individuals entitled and bound to pay such revenue. The first is done by demarcation and survey; the next by classification and assessment and the last by investigation and registration of titles. Thus prior to actual settlement is the work of Survey. When the surveyor has determined the position and size of every holding, the settlement officer enters the field and estimates the character of the soil, the kind of crop, the opportunities for irrigation, the present means of communication, their probable development, and all other circumstances which affect the value of the land and its produce.

The System of settlement obtaining in Travancore is the same that prevails in the Madras Presidency, (the Ryot wari system) according to which the ryots enjoy private ownership. and as such are made individually responsible to the state for payment of rent due from their holdings. On the other hand the old system of taxation under the village corporation as well as the Zemindary system, brought in by the Mahomedan rulers of India makes the head of the village corporation or the Zemindar, as the case may be, the representative of the ryots and accordingly the sole rent-paying agent. This system prevails largely in Bengal. It was however sought to be introduced in the Madras Presidency at the beginning of the last century when the country passed from the Nawab into the hands of the British. But owing to its utter failure and self-denying earnestness and enterprise of Sir Thomas Munro the Ryot warri system which will always be associated with his name came to be adopted and it was since 1858, the new survey and settlement were set on foot in Madras.

Dewan Seshia Sastri mentions that the earliest survey remembered by the oldest living accountant is that of 914 M. E. when Travancore was within its own ancient limits and remarks that the term is used in its broad sense as a Revenue Settlement which does not imply neccessarily a measurement of the land. It has been already remarked that after the series of brilliant conquests which resulted in the extension and consolidation of this state the credit of having organised for the first time an administrative machinery was due to the genius of Ramien Dhalawa. Mr. Shungunni Menon records in his history that the Maharajah having ordered Ramien Dhalawa to frame regular accounts and rules for fixing permanent taxes on land and gardens that officer commenced a survey of them in 926 M. E. and completed the laborious work throughout Travancore. The first Ayacut or assessment account was clearly framed out after this survey and the holders of the land and garden were furnished with a Pathivu or Registry. In 948 M. E., was made the next survey which embraced the whole of the garden lands and paddy fields. Sir Madhava Row in his unpublished manuscript of the history of the two sovereigns of Travancore immediately preceding the Maharajah under whom he served as Dewan, says that the general survey and assessment of landed properties instituted in 948 M. E. by the orders of the Maharajah disclosed to the state the individual possession of all holders. It is also to be noted, he continues, that all descriptions of land without respect to tenure came under this extraordinary impost which in the aggregate is said to have yielded about a lakh and seventy thousand Rupees. It was however like that of 929 M. E. an operation of mere Kandeluthu or what was heard from the ryots themselves in respect to the nature and extent of their holding and as such far from accurate. In 978 M.E. Velu Thampi who became Dewan by that time caused a survey of all lands and gardens. Unlike the previous operations this was one of Kandeluthu or what was seen, inspected and verified by Government Officers. The next survey was the operation of 990 M. E. under the Dalawaship of Dewan Padmanabhan. It introduced a system of classification which provided for different rates of assessment. During the administration of Diwan Subha Rao an attempt seems to have been made in 1012 M. E. In this a greater degree of system and fixity was attained. It provided for four distinct rates of assessment; also for tax both in kind as well as its commuted value in money. The rates of commutation however continued uneqnal and unfair. In 1040 M. E. a special survey agency seems to have been created. It confined its work only to coffee-estates and patches of cocoanut cultivation. In 1048 M. E. a survey of the town of Trivandrum alone was conducted and completed but no regular and systematic survey of the country under professional control and guidance was ever made. As observed by Dewan Rama Iyengar. "there was no record of the extent of the land, no classification of the soil, no systematic assessmeut, no register of titles, not even a complete rent roll or list of land-holders." The necessity of introducing a regular and compre hensive system of Revenue survey and settlement, as the groundwork for sound and successful administration came to be felt more and more. With this end in view all the principal land-holders of the country were invited to be a present at a meeting held at the capital on the 24th March 1883 at which the necessity and objects of the measure were thus explained :—

"The object of His Highness government in seeking to introduce a new survey and settlement is not so much to increase the Revenue as to ascertain the extent and resources of the country; to define and fix the boundaries of properties, to obtain accurate registers of land; to investigate and record the various tenures under which property is held: to fix and limit the Government demand; to equalise and not to enhance the pressure of the assessment on land; to remove the various anomalies which disfigure the Revenue administration, and press more or less upon the springs of industry; to give perfect freedom of action in taking up or relinquishing land; to impart perfect security of title to the holders and thus to promote the well-being of agricultural classes and the general prosperity of the state." The new Scheme was with the approval of the Madras Government introduced in 1883. It embraces all descriptions of land, cultivated and cultivable, occupied and unoccuped. The work is beng pushed on with all speed which expediency could suggest or the local condition would permit.

Other Measures:—A number of petty taxes which paralysed the energies of the ryots and afforded scope for oppression was remitted one after another, since these demands were found incompatible with present social and economical conditions. Forest regions are considerably opened up for cultivation. A good deal of waste lands near the ghats is reclaimed, Every facility is afforded to the development of planting industries.

The relation between landlords and tenants and the nature and extent of the rights each has over his holdings have engaged the attention of Goverment since 1042. M. E. By Royal proclamation of that year the tenants who held lands under certain terms were given permanent occupancy right over such lands. That proclamation however prescribed no convenient procedure for the recovery of rents. An elaborate enquiry was instituted into the rights of Jenmis (Lords) and Kudiyans (tenants). The result was the law passed in 1071 M. E. It settled many longstanding disputes and differences between the landlords and tenants.

In early times owing to the undeveloped state of inland trade, the absence of roads and other facilities of communication Govt. had to devise means to draw supplies by individual contributions from remote corners of the country for this purpose. A considerable portion of land is given as *inams* or free holds, in compensation for the services rendered. The holders of these lands were bound to supply provisions at nominal prices in connection with the religious and charitable institutions of the State. The substitution of a system of free labour and free supplies having been found suited to present conditions, the holders of those lands have been relieved from the heavy and onerous obligations attaching to the tenure. There was a practice that allowed garden lands to periodical inspection by Revenue authorities. If a single tree comes to bearing this year over and above the number of trees assessed last year, the Revenue authorities were at liberty to enter upon the property and assess that tree. This revision of assessment with reference to the number of additional taxable trees that come to bearing from time to time is known as *Kulachu Kooduthal.* This process was considered "so anomalous in its character, so questionable in principle and so discordant with the new system of revenue settlement," that it has now been totally abolished. The ryots are now perfectly free to improve their holdings and enjoy all the fruits of their improvement. In the interests of the agricultural population the Adiyara fees used to be levied in cases of the succession of distant kindred are abolished.

The ryots are permitted to reclaim lands adjoining the Ghats on very easy terms. Remission of taxes on failsure of crops is extended throughout the Kingdom. The procedure for the recovery of rents due to Government is systematised and simplified. In view to aid the ryots with loans of money from Government, a law has been passed by which the loan advanced may be repaid in convenient instalments. With the same end in view, agricultural exhibitions and cattle shows are held off and on. These are some of the several measures that have contributed to the fiscal growth of the country.

Law and Justice.—The foundation for a proper administration of justice was laid only in 1832. It appears from Mr. Shungunny Menon's History of Travancore that the reigning Prince at the time caused a code of Laws to be compiled after the model of the enactments in force in British territories, that this was the first code of regulations ever adopted and promulgated in Travancore and that described the constitution, powers and procedure of the Civil and Criminal Courts. The Dewan was the supreme Head of all the Departments and exercised Revenue, Police and Magisterial functions. Till 1871 the Dewan continued to be the chief Magistrate of the state. Before he was relieved of his judicial function, an important question of much political significance arose.

Jurisdiction over European British subjects. It relates to the arrangements as to jurisdiction over European British subjects.

The question of jurisdiction over them arose in connection with the trial of Mr. John Liddel, who was Commercial Agent of the Government at Alleppy. He stood charged with having embezzled a sum of Rs. 15,000 from the commercial Treasury with which he was entrusted. The Travancore Government tried him. For he was allowed to reside in Travancore on condition of his being subject to local laws. He had been residing in the state for a long time and acquired personal and landed property. He was actually a servant of the Travancore Government and bound by all obligations of a Government servant at the time of the commission of the offence. His offence was against Travancore Government. Further he was arrested in the country itself. And moreover he submitted to its jurisdiction. The Resident declared that none legally existed as defined by the published laws relating to Native States and referred the matter to Madras Government who as advised by Advocate General J. B. Norton arrived at the conclusion that under notification of the Governor-General of India in Council dated the 10th January 1867 in accordance with 28 Vic. 15th chapter, the trial of Mr. Liddel by the Travancore Government was *illegal*, that he might immediately be released and brought to trial before the Madras High Court". Sir Madhava Row who was Dewan at the time urged certain counter-considerations and arguments on the general question. He contended that jurisdiction was an inherent right, that the Travancore state being ruled by its own ruler possessed that right, that it has not been shown by British Government that Travancore has ceded this right and that the Governor-General's notification relied upon by Mr. Norton did not mean to deprive Travancore of that right but only distributed what right the British Government had over its own subjects residing out of British territory. The proceedings of the Madras Government with reference to this protest declared that "the trial of Mr. Liddel by the Travancore Government is notwithstanding his personal waiver a nullity and that the proclamation of the Governor-General does not confer upon the High Court a concurrent jurisdiction with the courts of Travancore. It takes away from these courts jurisdiction over British subjects, being Europeans and Christians and confers an exclusive jurisdiction over such class upon the High Court."

Sir Madhava Row sought and obtained the legal advice of Mr. John D. Mayne. He maintained that Travancore has never been conquered by the East India Company and has never surrendered its sovereignty to the Company or the Queen that none of the treaties with the Travancore Rajah contemplate any abandonment of his territorial jurisdiction, that the treaty of 1805 did not supersede but merely supplement the Treaty of 1795, that it provided that in an event which has never occurred, the British Government might assume the Government of Travancore, that till that event occurs, the Rajah's rights of internal Government remain unimpaired, that though clause 9 of the Treaty of 1805 binds the Rajah "to pay at all times the utmost attention to such advice as the E glish Government shall occasionally offer him with a view to the administration of justice" this does not entail the English Government to supersede the Rajah's courts or to deprive them of any part of their Jurisdiction which by the law of nations they possess, that the Governor-General's proclamation could not of course go beyond the powers given by the statute and the statute, though binding on all British subjects, has of course no force against the sovereign of Travancore and that he fully agreed with Sir Madhava Row that neither the statute nor the Proclamation conplated any such interference by the Government. This opinion was forwarded to the Government of Madras who appointed a committee for the purpose. They upheld Mr. Mayne's view on which Mr. Norton wrote. "On further consideration and with the advantage of weighing all that has been urged by the President and members, the Dewan and my learned friend Mr. Mayne, I have come to the conclusion that the trial of Liddel by the Travancore Government is legal and therefore he ought to be left to undergo the remainder of his sentence." The order of the Government of Madras was as follows:—"In acordance with this opinion, His Excellency the Governor in Council sees no reason for questioning the legality of the sentence passed on Liddel by Travancore and resolves therefore to cancel the order of Government."

When the jurisdiction of Travancore was recognised there were difficulties in the way. They were removed by legislation which brought about an alteration in the existing practice. The Government of India decided in 1874 that "His Highness' Magistrates who are European British subjects and Christians may exercise over European British subjects the same Jurisdiction as may be exercised over them in British India by European British subjects who are Magistrates of the 1st class and Justices of the Peace." We have special Magistrates and a special appellate Judge appointed accordingly who are empowered to commit to the High Court at Madras such cases as in British territories are beyond the jurisdiction of European British subjects who are Magistrates of the 1st class and Justices of the Peace. It is stipulated further that these arrangements are subject to revision if at any time the European Magistrates of these states fail to give satisfaction to the British Government. Independent Judicial tribunals were established since then and the courts were reconstituted in 1882, after the British Indian model. During the present reign a number of Regulations has been passed which have further strengthend and improved the machinery for the administration of Justice.

The Legislative Council:—Of the several reforms initiated since the accession of the present Maha-Rajah the most important is the institution of the Legislative Council in 1888. The value of the measure will be enhanced by the fact that among all the Native States of India, Travancore is the first to recognise it as an indispensable adjunct to a civilized and enlightened Government. In former days the term Act or Regulation was unknown and all the measures of the state were promulgated by Royal proclamations. Now the Legislative Council gives full and free scope for the play of cultivated intelligence and enlightened public opinion. It certainly marks a turning point in the history of Travancore. The constitution of the Council is laid down by Regulation 5 of 1073 M. E. which is an adaptation of the Indian Councils Act of 1892. Speaking to the South Travancoreans H. H. the Maharajah said:—" I am glad that you appreciate the Legislative Council recently inaugurated. The presence of non-official members in it is I trust some guarantee that the wishes of the people will be represented at the deliberations of the Council:" With reference to the same His Highness observed elsewhere " the world moves forward and we must move on with it or it will leave us behind. In this latter part of the 19th century neither princes nor people can afford to ignore this progressive tendency."

These extracts show the enlightened zeal of

the Maharajah to advance with the progressive spirit of the age.

Police.—Prior to 1881 there was no distinctly organised Police in Travancore. The function of the Police was combined with that of Magistrates. Such a combination was found as objectionable in principle as it was inconvenient in practice. Accordingly a complete separation of the Police and Magistracy was effected and a clear line of demarcation drawn between the judicial function of the Magistrate and the preventive and detective duties of the Police. A separate Police force was instituted on the lines of the Police organisation in British India. The members of the force were enlisted from all classes with due regard to age and physical fitness and placed under the immediate control of a European Superintendent. They were so equipped and trained as to be available for employment in any part of the country. The only hardship they had of contributing to the superannuation fund has now been removed by the extension to them of the benefit of pension or gratuity according to the period of their service. Another recent measure of reform is the replacement of the system of anthropometrical measurements by the system of identification by means of finger impressions. The country is free from any violent crime. This is due to the peaceful habits of the people no less than the preventive and detective capacity of the Police force. Mr. Bensely who has been at the head of the force since its organisation is not guilty of any exaggeration when he writes:—"There is security of life and property throughout the country and upon the roads and waterways to an extent unknown in the surrounding British Districts of Madura, Tinnevelly and Malabar."

Prisons.—Though rules were passed from time to time to improve this class of Institutions of which there are three in the State—a Central Jail and two District Jails, the former under the control of a trained Superintendent and the latter under the control of the District Magistrates within whose jurisdiction they are—there was till quite recently no recognised law relating thereto. It was in 1895 that the Prisons Regulation was passed on the basis of the British enactment. Since then better discipline is maintained: unwholesome food is prohibited: cleanliness is rigorously enforced: and over-crowding is prevented. The Juvenile offenders are separated from hardened convicts, and given, in the Reformatory School a training which would blot out the evil influence of their early life. The increase of mortality among the convicts has led to the organization of a committee to investigate the subject and on their recommendations, steps are being taken to minimise the death rate. A Jail manufactory is maintained, where every facility is thrown open for convict labour such as weaving cloth, making coir, printing and varied other useful industrial works. The regulation also provides for the release of convicts who are, in a precarious state of health. They are released under sanction of H. H. the Maharajah in the exercise of the Royal Prerogative of mercy. The Brahmin convicts are exempted from hard labour owing to the peculiar custom and social usages of the people and so are female convicts of whatever class. Both these classes of convicts are for the same reason immuned from capital punishment. The regulation also provides for a scale of revised dietary for convicts. Special diets are given to foreign and sick convicts. Destitute convicts are given travelling fare on their release.

Registration.—This Department also was thoroughly reorganized and reformed in 1070 M. E. The old system was superseded by Regulation I of that year. According to that system the work of registration was done by an agency of village notaries who were appointed and controlled by the Sadr Court. These notaries were not given any fixed salary but remunerated by fees levied upon instruments registered by them. This unpaid agency was a source of dissatisfaction to the public, delay in work and loss to Government. Registration under the old system made no difference between the properties registered and not registered, for it left the registration or non-registration to the option of the parties concerned. The result was a tendency in favor of non-registration. This tendency was accelerated by the interposition of the village notaries themselves. Consequently in 1042 M. E. this system was superseded by a new legislation under which the Registrars became the paid servants of the State and a separate staff of these servants was organized and graded according to quantity of work assigned to them. According to the new Regulation, free scope was given for the registration of deeds relating to moveable property also. Even this system was found wanting. It was revised and improved in 1052 M. E. by a Regulation passed in that year. It removed much hardship and inconvenience and many sources of uncertainty and loss. In view to impart additional security for the fulfilment of contracts, the system was thoroughly reformed again in 1070 M. E. under a Regulation based on the latest British Act. In fact every step has been taken by H. H's Government to secure the chief object of Registration which is "to give certainty of titles and to prevent the operation of fraudulent and secret transactions by which a man's right in property which he has acquired may be defeated."

The instruments of protection are so far placed within the easy reach of the people that there are every where signs of the stability of the State and the happiness of the people. A vast net work of excellent roads has made travel a recreation. White-walled Bungalows, crown the top of wealthy hills which were once considered inaccessible. Pepper from Quilon, ginger from Palai and tea from Poonmudi are daily exchanged in the markets of Trivandrum. Long strings of bullock carts heavy with the products of the country, pass securely through forests where once the fierce tiger and the mighty elephant were the lords of all they surveyed. Huge bridges span over ; fords and rivers. The introduction of the Police and a better administration of Criminal justice have made the bold sons of Kayankulum Kochunni and Mulagmood Adimai understand that hunger should be satisfied not by rapine but by industry. The reform of the Registration Department and the reconstitution of the Civil Courts have taught the people that their difference should be settled not by blows but by arbitration. Is it then strange that Governor after Governor was, like Lord Ampthill "impressed with the happy smiles of a peaceful and contented people?"

CHAPTER IV—ECONOMIC GROWTH.

Owing to the short-comings of the previous settlements, the method of collecting taxes and keeping accounts was in a shapeless condition, the village accounts—the corner-stone of a state's finance and the back-bone of all administrative systems were not kept under any regular form or strict provision. No two Taluqs resembled each other in their village accounts. Each Taluq had a separate method peculiar to itself, often changing with the change of accountants In Shencotta for instance a Rupee received was valued at and entered as 8 fanams, while a Rupee spent was worth only 7 fanams. In Nanchanaud, the accounts showed a collection higher than the actual. The difference was understood to be accounted for by a difference in the rate of commutation. The system of *Ezuthithircha* and *tirattu* were the direct outcome of these irregularities. The confusion was such that it eluded analysis and defied all powers of description. Several improvements have been made within the last 17 years in the system of accounts. The preparation of estimates of income and expenditure in the form obtaining in the Madras Presidency has for the most part been adopted . In fact several changes have been introduced on the lines of the British system. With every anxiety to improve further the system of accounts, a Committe was recently organized to examine the system thoroughly and minutely and suggest means of further improvement. It is a remarkable fact that the financial condition of the state has during the period under review been one of steady advancement and the surplus revenue is used in developing the resources of the country and contributing to the welfare of the people. We shall now advert to the sources of income and the directions of outlay.

Forests:—We have already noticed that Travancore is covered with an abundance of superb forests. The forest revenue is therefore considerable. It is derived from the toll on and the sale of timber, and from forest produce such as cardamom, dammer, wax, honey, ivory etc. Formerly trees were felled down under a permit. But this indiscriminate felling gave a rude shock to the balance provided by nature. Seeds were brought down from Nilgiris and a systematic attempt was made for replenishing the exhausted forests. Several measures were taken to develop the forest revenue. The log system was introduced in supersession of the practice of levying tolls according to the cubical contents of the timber. This was followed by a grazing fee on cattle coming from the British side. Private persons were allowed to cut down timber on payment of tariff rates. But there was till recently no law to reserve forests. In view to organize a scheme of systematic conservancy and reproduction, a Regulation was passed in 1888 which provided ample scope to replenish the forests and to meet the demand for timber. In 1893 this Regulation was further revised and replaced by a more comprehensive one based on the British Indian Forest Act. Among the several changes brought about under the provisions of the amended regulation, the exclusive departmental working of the forests is one. It has superseded the permit system which left the collection and transporation o timber to private agencies. The forest area is cut up for purpose of control into several divisions and ranges and with a view to place them as far as possible under men trained in scientific forestry, Government have provided for young men being sent from time to time to study in the forest school of the Government of India at Dehra Dun—a step which was.warmly approved by Lord Curzon during his visit to this state.

Cardamom and other goods:—In the High Ranges there are some elevated plains where cardamom grows luxuriantly. This tract is mostly within the limits of the Thodupuzha Taluk. Cardamom, like pepper, is an important indigenous product and was a state monopoly. The cardamom Hills were also controlled and managed by the Conservator of forests till 1044 M. E. In that year, the supervision of the hills was transferred to a separate officer appointed for the purpose. The tract was leased out to the ryots who had to deliver the produce to Government at a fixed valuation. The ryots cultivated cardamom and received 2/5 of the sale proceeds. Fresh facilities of communication tended to the extension of the area of cultivation. As the system of monopoly was not found to work well, it was abolished in 1896. With the introduction of landtax, the ryots enjoy almost the rights of permanent occupancy as well as of giving up the holdings at will. This has created greater interest in the raising and collection of the produce,

Salt:—A brief history of this may be summarised as follows from a state memorandum on the subject.

" The history of the salt Department in Travancore may be divided into 2 periods, one preceding the monopoly and the other subsequent to its institution in the year 908. M. E.

The Travancore Government appears to have derived a revenue from salt so early as the middle of the last century, but there was at that time clearly no monopoly of any kind. The manufacture was apparently free and unrestricted and subject to but one fiscal regulation—namely, that the salt produced should be divided between the Government and the ryot in the same manner as paddy grown on rice lands. The salt was manufactured at certain seaside stations between Cape Comorin and Colachel, and in the margin of the backwaters in Trivandrum, Sherayinkil, Karthigapully, aud Karunagapally Taluqs, the seaside manufactories being known as Ullums, and the back-water ones as

Padanays. The salt made at the former was better in quality than the latter, being white in colour and comparatively free from impurities while the other was dark and mixed with earthy particles. It consequently fetched a higher price in the market. The salt pans were either the property of Government, or of private individuals. As already stated, the s lt produced was divided between the Government and the manufacturer, in certain fixe l proportion varying according to the nature of the ownership in the pans but the exact ratio cannot he ascertained at this distance of time. The Government share of the produce appears to have been taken over by servants told off for the purpose and sold on the spot, as I can find no trace of its having been stored or removed to any selling depots.

The entire quantity produced fell considerably short of the demand for home consumption and the deficit was made good by importation by private traders from Goa and Bombay and other ports.

It was in the year 988 M E. that the existing state of things was put an end to and a close monopoly introduced under a proclamation signed by Col. Munro who was then both Resident and Dewan. By that Proclamation all manufacture by the ryots except on Government account. A special department was organized for the superintendence and collection of the salt Revenue. Salt depöts were established in various parts of the country to place the article within the reach of the people and to facilitate sale and what was produced in the country was supplemented by import from abroad. From the year 989. M. E. to 1037, there was nothing of importance done, beyond the occasional abolition or re-opening of certain selling depots. Up to the year 1036 all wastage in the transport of salt by sea from the southern pans to the northern sale depots was charged to the manufacturer, but in that year the Government undertook to bear all loss from wastage. The negotiations in connection with the Interportal Convention which took place in 1865 had been going on for some time between the Travancore and British Governments, and *inter alia* the question of the adoption of the British Indian monopoly selling price of salt by this state was fully discussed and decided in the affirmative. In the year 1040 M. E. in which the convention was concluded, this Government accordingly raised its selling price and has since raised and lowered it with each successive rise and fall in the British Indian rate. As another result of this convention the salt pans on the banks of back-waters in central Travancore had to be closed. The sites of the old salt beds have since been converted into cocoanut topes for which the soil is better adapted than for salt. The next important step taken for improving the salt department was the substitution of weights for measures in all salt transactions, and this was introduced in the latter part of the year 1051. Another equally important one was the introduction of the bagging system, under which the scope for petty thefts and adulteration which used to be common in the case of salt transit from the stores to the selling depots has very much diminished." In 1058 the salt department was placed under the management of a separate officer. The salt consumption in the country averages 6 lacs of Indian maunds. It continues to be a state monopoly and sold in Government Bankshalls. Regulation III of 1063 which is an adaptation of the Madras Act provides for the manufacture and sale of salt. *Opium and bhang* are also state monopolies whose importation and sale are governed by Regulation VI of 1063 M. E.

Tobacco was formerly a strict state monopoly. The high character of the monopoly rates and the temptation they offered to practise contraband trade, not, to speak of other evils led to the abolition of the monopoly. It is allowed to be imported by all persons subject to certain restrictions. Regulation II of 1890 governs the importation and sale of this commodity of which there are 4 varieties. The equalisation of the duties since 1896 has swept away the evils consequent upon the difference in duties which existed before that period.

Abkari—The revenue derived from this was administered on the farming system till 1898. According to this system the monopoly of selling toddy and country liquor was knocked down,

Taluq by Taluq to the highest bidder. This system however was discontinued under the new Abkari. Regulation passed in that year. It introduced what is known as the Excise system experimentally in one Taluq. It was extended to a whole division in the following year since the experiment has so far proved a success. Sixty years ago the Abkari Revenue amounted to 40,000 Rs. per annum. It was fluctuating between that sum and 50,000 Rs. up to 1033. In 1060 M. E .it rose to 3 and odd lacs of Rupees and in 1075 it has gone up to over 6 lacs of Rupees or in other words 12 times the yield in 1033. This increase in revenue is due to effective prevention of contraband trade.

Medical Relief:—The directions of outlay are vast and varied. About 60 years ago there was only one medical institution in the State. The present Civil Hospital in Trivandrum was opened in 1865 by the Maharajah in person. The following extract from the address delivered by His Highness on that occasion is worthy of reproduction:—

" From time out of mind, charity has been regarded by Travancore as one of the cardinal duties of the State. Its reputation as Dharma Raj is familiar to all India. What can be more real, more substantial charity, than the provision of means for the relief or mitigation of sickness and disease ?

I hope that this institution will be freely resorted to by those for whom it is designed, and that it will be always distinguished for its sanitary arrangements, for the attention and tender care of the sick and suffering, and for the successful accomplishment of its main end—the cure of disease.

It is intended to train in this institution a body of intelligent and hard-working young men destined to carry into the interior the benefits of European medical Science and Arts.

One of the main objects of my ambition is to see that good medical aid is placed within the reach of all classes of my subjects. It is a blessing which is not at present in the power of individuals generally to secure, how-much-soever they may desire it. It is hence the obvious duty of this State to render its assistance in this direction.

Turning to the building at which we are assembled, I view it with some pride and satisfaction. I trust that it is the fore-runner of many useful institutions, whether designed to cure disease, to facilitate the administration of the Government in its several departments or to impart knowledge and wisdom."

These sanguine anticipations are now more than fulfilled. Medical institutions are dotted all over the country. There is one Government institution within every square of 12 miles. And in view to supplement the Medical Service afforded by Government institutions, and to promote the practice of medicine by private agency, medical grants are given to Hospitals, Dispensaries and native medical practitioners. Medical Scholarships are awarded to students for the study of medicine in the European Universities. The encouragement of the study of medicine among women and the institution of Women and Children's Hospital and the rapid expansion of medical relief in general belong to the last seventeen years.

Sanitation:—Till the year 1894 there was no Regulation to provide for the Conservancy and Sanitation of towns. Rules and orders passed from time to time served the purpose. It was in that year that a Regulation based on the Punjab Muncipal Act was passed "to provide for the better Sanitation of towns, the prevention of fires and the Registration of births and deaths." Its working is controlled by a local body called the Town Improvement Committee composed of official and non-official members. This Regulation was further amended in 1901 so as to provide for a comprehensive scheme for the maintenance of general sanitation and the reconstitution of the Committee on a more representative basis. As observed by the late Mr. Thanu Pillai who introduced the bill which has now become law, "It is an important measure. Though generally built upon the existing organisation, it has a deeper foundation and a wider scope than the present law. It is in fact the first real step towards Muncipal action proper. In the constitution, powers and responsibilities of the

Committee and in other important points there is a distinct onward move." Under the Towns Conservancy Regulation, a special Department was organised " embracing vaccination, vital statistics, rural sanitation and itinerant medical relief."

Public Works; The prosecution in a systematic manner of several works of public utility throughout the length and breadth of the land, commenced with the appointment of Mr. Barton as Chief Engineer. Several roads were opened, numerous bridges were built and many imposing and handsome buildings were constructed. Dewan Seshia Sastri has placed on record " the great zeal and untiring energy with which Mr. Barton has labored and successfully brought to completion works that will do lasting credit to his name. " His successors have also utilized their engineering talents for which there was full and free scope. More roads are opened, existing roads are repaired and metalled. Torrent streams are bridged, channels are widened and deepened, tanks are scooped out. In fact the operations embrace engineering works of a varied character requiring professional skill such as new Irrigation schemes.

Irrigation. The most successful area of land that exists in Travancore for the cultivation of rice is in the southern tracts. Artificial irrigation is therefore most needed there. A special agency to conduct the irrigation works seems to have been in existence as far back as 1010 M. E. This was however. absorbed in the Engineer's Department soon after its organisation. Among the several important irrigation works may be mentioned the construction of the Pandian and Puthan dams which divert the waters of the Paralayar into the valleys of the southern tracts. The demand for water having exceeded this supply, attention was directed to divert the Kothayar waters for the purpose.

Colonel Mead R. E. whose services were lent to the State by the Madras Government thought that "until something is known of the amount of water available in the rivers by means of gauges, nothing should be done, and most certainly nothing should be attempted until the question as to what is to be done with the Kothayar water is settled." He estimated the cost of the Kothayar Project at 6 lacs of Rs. at the least, and said that in the absence of water Registers, he was unable to agree with the then Chief Engineer in urging upon His Highness' Government to undertake this work at once.

Acting on these views, the then Dewan Ramiengar directed that the Kothayar scheme should lie over till full and complete data were available. This was in 1057 M. E. In 1061 M. E. the Chief Engineer wrote as follows to His Highness' Government: "The cutting of a channel from the Kothayar at *Thiruparappu* was not proposed by me; the scheme I fear cannot be thought of owing to its costliness and the small result obtainable."

We quote here the forcible remarks of the Resident Mr. Rees.—" Irrigation works properly so-called, exist only in the Southern division and the whole of the above sums, with the exception of Rupees 5941, was spent in that division, the large excess under repairs in 1072 being due to works in connection with the closing of breaches caused by heavy floods. The original estimate for this project intended to irrigate an area of about 50000 acres amounted to Rs. 7,94,850. It was subsequently considered that an area could be irrigated of 70000 acres and though revenue investigations to prove this point and to investigate local conditions and revenue prospects of the larger scheme are not, I understand, complete, an estimate amounting to 19 lacs, has been prepared. The Durbar has so far taken unofficially, I believe, the advice of Mr. Walch as well as that of its Chief Engineer; but in regard to so large a scheme, in respect of which estimates may be greatly exceeded, the Durbar would wish, I know, that *a second opinion* should be officially taken before His Highness' Government is finally committed to the larger scheme which now holds the field. I visited the work in January last. Inasmuch as the Northern divisions have few artificial irrigation works, the material Channels, which are in many cases silted up or in need of repair should, I think, not escape attention, while the South adds to its present irrigation systems *this ambitious scheme of damming the Kothayar river.*"

Railway :—The construction of a light railway has been long in contemplation and schemes from time to time were investigated and surveys of the line made. That since his accession, His Highness the present Maharajah was very anxious to bring about the speedy extension of the Railway communication into the heart of Travancore so as to develop its natural resources, is evident from the following passage in a speech to the inhabitants of Tinnevelly in 1888: "My Government was in correspondence with the South Indian Railway Company regarding the extension of the line into Travancore. We have not yet heard from the Company in reply and I may assure you that I am equally desirous to have the Railway extended to Travancore." He said elsewhere: "I hope the time is not distant when the Railway will bind us together in closer ties.". It was in 1893 that, at the instance of the Government of India, a final survey was made of the extension of the South Indian Railway to Quilon at the cost of the Durbar and since its completion, negotiations were opened for the commencement of the line by the South Indian Railway Company to whom a sum of 17 lacs of Rupees has been advanced without interest for carrying on the work. Lands have been assumed for the line which is close upon completion. Lord Ampthill anticipates the prosperity of the people as favourably affected by this line when at Tuticorin His Excellency remarked: "When the Tinnevelly-Quilon

Railway is completed, there is a great possibility of the development of trade in Travancore." He added that Tuticorin "may reasonably hope to attract a considerable proportion of export trade from Travancore which will find there an improved outlet."

Trade :—It is a remarkable fact that more than 88 per cent of the trade of Travancore is with British India and this has been mainly due to the removal of the fiscal restrictions between Travancore and British India according to the Interportal Convention of 1865. The arrangements which were submitted by the Madras Government as regards Travancore were : the free admission of all goods, the produce or manufacture of India except cotton and cotton goods, metals, tobacco, salt, opium and spirits ; the free admission of all goods, the produce or manufacture of Travancore into British India, with the exception of Salt, Opium and spirits ; the adoption of British Indian rates of duty on all foreign goods imported into Travancore except the articles above-mentioned ; the levy of duties not less than those obtaining in British India on exports ; the adoption of British Indian tariff valuation, the export tariff being taken in regard to cotton fabrics of native manufacture : and the adoption of British Indian monopoly price of salt. The Government of India did not accede to the exception stipulated for by Travancore in respect of import duty on raw and manufactured and crude and manufactured metals, whether British Indian or foreign (including English) which have paid duty at British Indian ports or have been exempted from duty on exportation from thence or in respect of the reservation of rights to levy export duty on every article of its own produce whither-so-ever exported. The effect of the first of these was to place the British staples of piece goods and metals under a disadvantage while they were imported into Travancore. Notwithstanding that all articles of Travancore produce are manufactured, all foreign articles re-exported from Travancore ports would be admitted duty free into British Indian ports and the effect of the second was to enable the Travancore Government to levy high export duties at the cost of British interests, because if import duty were charged in British Indian ports on such export, Travancore Government could not charge such high rates of export duty.

Accordingly the Travancore Government were asked to reconsider and revise the proposals. After a lengthened controversy and correspondence the Travancore Government agreed to abolish the first and lower the tariff rate on the second. The Madras Government accepted the proposals and got them confirmed by the Government of India and the final arrangement then made in respect of the removal of fiscal restrictions on trade between Travancore and British India obtains to this day.

The removal of fiscal restrictions and the facilities of communication have given a fresh impetus to industrial pursuits and the result is the steady economic growth of the country,

CHAPTER V.

EDUCATION, SCIENCE AND ART.

Education in Travancore, presents five different periods in the history of its progress. The first period dates from 1836, the year that followed the close of the memorable and acrimonious controversy for more than two decades between English and Oriental learning, to which the educational enactment of 1813 gave rise. The decision in favour of the Anglicists, influenced mostly by Lord Macaulay's famous minute of 1835, was quickly and eagerly taken advantage of by the Travancore Government which welcomed the first representative of the New Education in the person of Mr. Roberts, "the Pioneer of English Education in Travancore." Reference to this early attempt to catch the glimpse of Western enlightenment is made in the following extract from Mr. Nagam Aiya's excellent Census Report:—"Even before the University was founded, Trivandram maintained a High School teaching up to the standard not much below the present B. A. and as such was inferior only to the Educational centres of the Presidency towns. All the high officers of the State, including the present and retired Dewans, have been educated in this High School, and the service of Travancore, it is said and said with just pride, contains more English educated people than any other town in the Presidency excepting Madras." The famous despatch of 1854 by Sir C. Wood (afterwards Lord Halifax) which has been rightly called the Magna Charta of education in India marks the beginning of the second period in the history of education in Travancore. From that time the progress made was immense. In his unceasing efforts to carry out the policy of his worthy predecessor, Mr. Bensley obtained such marked results, and won the honest affection of his pupils to such an extent that he is to this day remembered as "the popular and conscientious schoolmaster."

The third and most important period corresponds with the establishment of Indian Universities in the tumults of the Mutiny of 1857. It was then that a regular and comprehensive system of education was organised and promotion of education formally and liberally recognised as a duty of Government. A net-work of institutions was extended over the country far and wide, graduated from the District English School to the highest College. And fortunately an eminent educationest, decidedly the best that Travancore has had, came out from "Modern Athens." The triumphant issue of the yeoman service which Mr. Ross rendered to the country in the cause of education won for him a worthy tribute from the Maharaja, of the appellation of "the master-tiller of the intellectual soil of Travancore." Under the subsequent stewardship of his talented countryman and veteran educationist Dr. Harvey, Higher Education stepped further to the fore-front in the fourth period of its history. Dr. Harvey reigned as head and leader of the educational forces for over seven years and was to the Travancoreans for more than twenty years literally a guide, philosopher and friend. The Trivandram College rose to such a high distinction that there existed a sort of honest and laudable rivalry between it and the Kumbakonam College which was at the time in many respects one of the best educational institutions in the Madras Presidency. With reference to this satisfactory state of the college, His crudite Highness, the late Maharajah, observed in the course of His Highness' presidential address at the distribution of annual prizes in the Kumbakonam College:—"You refer to my College at Trivandram. It is doing good work under able and earnest professors and teachers and will, I hope, long continue to hold its own in the race for the advancement of Higher Education." Again Mr. Powell whose name is a watchword, writing in 1834 to Sir Henry Roscoe to ask him to recommend an eligible man for the Professorship of Chemistry said of this College:—"The College has had considerable success, as my former position of Director of Public Instruction for the Madras Presidency enabled me to ascertain."

It was under a combination and succession of turning circumstances such as these that the fifth period commenced its operations. Agreeably to the principles laid down by the Education commission of Lord Ripon's Government to complete the scheme inaugurated in 1854, His illustrious Highness, the late Royal Savant, made a bold and happy stroke to introduce the study of natural sciences in the Trivandram College. The glorious result was the memorable advent of that social Professor of versatile genius, Mr. Read, whose departure is deeply deplored.

"In 1894 the Educational Department was thoroughly re-organised, the dual control over the systems of Veranoular and English education was abolished, and all schools, English and Vernacular, were, for purposes of admimistration and inspectoral control, placed under three Range Inspectors in direct correspondence with Government. The chief educational institutions at the capital—the Arts Colleges for boys and girls, the Law College, the Sanskrit College, the Normal school, the Industrial school of Arts and the Agricultural Demonstration Farm—remained, however, as before in charge of their respective heads. A Code of Rules known as the "Travancore Educational rules" and a revised "grant-in-aid Code" were passed. In the matter of grants-in-aid, the policy of Government has been to utilise private effort, with due regard to efficiency to foster and to encourage it, to supplement it where it fails to adequately meet requirements, and to supply its place where it does not exist. Acting on this principle, Government have refrained from opening schools where private schools capable of meeting local requirements exist, and have freely started schools in districts which, from an educational point of view, are backward."

If there is one area of legislative and administrative activity where something may be done for raising the status and conducing to the welfare of the people, it is in the sphere of Education. The statesman wants to know if the people are trained in intelligence to hold their own in competiton with other nations in the world. The parents are concerned to ascertain that their children are receiving the best education that can be got and will be of great aid in the struggle for existence. The establishment of four Arts Colleges, and a Law College, the only other institution of its kind existing in South India, prove beyond doubt the exalted importance attached to and the extensive demand for higher education. A colonial Statesman has said that such institutions are really fortresses of civilization. There are in Travancore over 2000 such fortresses of varied size and dispositions. The organization of Training schools to impart instruction in the theory and practice of teaching: of Agricultural schools to diffuse elementary knowledge of agriculture: of Industrial schools to teach Arts works and of Medical and Survey schools, give unerring evidence of the broader and more popular basis on which public instruction has been placed. It will not be out of place to mention that technical enterprise and indigenous talents are adequately recognised and largely encouraged. We have only to point to the Technical and Medical scholarships awarded by His Highness' Government to enable Travancore students to undergo training in Europe also special scholarships for training students in Forestry etc.— a most gratifying feature as it is a conspicuous proof of the enlightened spirit which always animates the benign ruler of the state.

Female Education :— Another fact worthy of prominent mention is the marked advancement of female education in Travancore. The prejudices of the people have been overcome and all artificial restraints removed from the acquirement of knowledge by women. Under the noble policy of liberal education pursued by its enlightened ruler, Travancore has even stolen a march on British India. What with gosha system and the early marriage of Hindu girls, the opportunities for female higher education are very limited. But in Travancore it has come to such a standard of advancement that the country has long taken the foremost position in India. Even so far back as 1857 the nucleus of a girl's school was formed under the superintendence of Miss Abel. She was succeeded by Miss Mainwaring. It is recorded that her management "has been increasingly creditable alike to herself, beneficial in a high degree to the people and gratifying to His Highness' Government." Her successor was Miss Donnelly. She was long connected with the institution. She worked hard and she worked well and did much for the expansion of female education. High caste native girls began to join the institution which was originally confined to christian girls. The institution prospered much under her creditable stewardship. It rose to the standard of a High school. Through the unceasing efforts and enterprise of her sucessor, Miss Williams, it has expanded still further. It has risen to the status of a second grade College and is affiliated to the Madras University. It is very gratifying to find that even earlier than the beginning of the College for boys there was an institution maintained under the auspices of the zenana mission in Europe. This institution was and continues to be chiefly confined to the education of High caste Hindu girls.

His Highness' Government assists it by a free house and a large grant. Miss Blandford who was from its inception connected with the institution has worked hard with remarkable zeal to improve it. Schools for girls are dotted all over the country and those who wish to continue their studies for higher diplomas can do so in the Government girls' College or the Convent College which under the watchful care of the Lady superior is flourishing well. When Lord Curzon recently honored the country with a visit the sight that pleased him most was the vast array of bright-eyed Student girls who were called together to receive him and of the several acts of the adminitration which he commended much, one was the generous help given by His Highness in the cause of female emancipation.

Side by side with this, the enlightenment of the backward classes is steadily maintained. The institution of a scheme of public lectures and of Educational Boards have done much to extend the advantages of popular education The exlightened zeal of the sovereign has shown itself active in mantaining a Sanskrit College to develop a system of classical education in sanskrit which is unrivalled for the intellectual subtilty of resources.

Museum. It was in 1843 that General Cullen wrote and submitted to Madras Government a memorandum strongly urging the advantages and desirability of establishing local museums. About 1852 Mr. J. A. Broun, the Astronomer and Geologist who is well known by his meteorological observations arrived in Trivandrum. In him General Cullen found a distinguished scientific coadjutor. Shortly after his arrival, it was proposed to start in Trivandrum "a museum of objects illustrative of the natural and physical sciences, of the arts and of the products and antiquities of Travancore as a means of aiding the natives in their efforts to gain a practical knowledge of the arts and sciences of Europe and of preserving the rapidly decaying illustrations of the ancient manners and customs of the country." In 1854 the Madras Government communicated to General Cullen their approval of his scheme generally. Accordingly a society was formed in 1855 with H. H. The Maha Rajaha as Patron, General Cullen as President and Mr. Broun as Secretary. It was however only in 1857 that the Museum was thrown open to the public and it is gratifying to note that so many as 3000 persons visited it that year. One remarkable feature was that of this number 10 per cent. were women. The Museum became a Government Institution since 1859 when, a substantial grant was allowed under Mr. Broun's successors. The collections increased and with it the popularity of the institution increased likewise. In 1873 the foundation of a new building was laid by H. H. The Maha Rajah and a sum of Rs 70000 was sanctioned for the work. It was designed by Mr. Chisholm the talented consulting architect of the Madras Government. In 1880 the collections were removed to a new building which was completed by that time. It is called the Napier Museum after the name of and as a compliment to the then Governor of Madras. The institution was placed under the management of a committee with the Resident as president. Col. Ketchen who continued as Honorary Secretary till 1889 did much for the development of the institution. Mr. H. S. Ferguson who succeeded him, was, when the committee was abolished in 1894, appointed Director. During his connection with the institution he has made systematic collections of new species of fauna. In his own words "we have most of our mammals represented in our museum, a good proportion of birds, all the snakes and nearly all the amphibia. The butterflies are pretty complete. And we have large collections of the other orders of insects. The art collections are progressing. Cases representing the ivory carving, brass work, lace, wood-carving, kuft gari work, are all complete. The hill tribes are represented with all their peculiar instruments. A good collection of the musical instruments of the country had been made with some care and trouble. But they were sent on loan to one of the London exhibitions."

Public gardens. This also owes its existence to the efforts and endeavours of Mr. Broun. The project was taken up in 1859. Several plants and flowers were reared and cuttings of many were procured from Bangalore and other places. Attached to the garden is also a collection of animals. Some of these were presented by General Cullen. Others were presented by H. H. the Maharajah who like other Indian potentates kept a private menagerie. A large allotment was given in 1863 for making cages for these animals. Major Davidson who was in charge of the Gardens expressed the hope that in process of time "they will reach such a state of perfection as not only to rival the Lalbagh at Bangalore and the Agri-Horticultural gardens and people's park in Madras but also to remain a constant evidence of that great regard for the general interests of his own subjects no less than of the British residents merely in his dominions, that has always been evinced by H. H. the Maharajah and by the Government of Travancore." His anticipations have been more than fulfilled. In 1891 Mr. Ingleby who had been trained at Kew, was appointed Superintendent and he held that office for 6 years during which time the garden labour was systematically organized and brought to bear upon its steady improvement. Mr Ferguson who has now sole charge of the Public gardens Department has made further improvements. He works with great zeal and vigour to develop the institutions under his charge—institutions in which he takes a most lively interest.

Observatory. We have elsewhere referred to the observatory established at Trivandram in 1836. The first meteorological observations were recorded by John Caldecott who was appointed Astronomer of the state and commissioned to furnish the institution with the best instruments. He continued till 1849 and was succeeded by Mr. Broun in 1852. It was during his time the most extensive observations were recorded. A branch Observatory was established on the top of the Agastya peak in 1855. It however fell to pieces during his absence and was finally abolished. On his return to Europe, Mr. Broun was engaged in publishing his observations for a number of years. The institution has received a new lease of life with the advent of Dr. Mitchell, a Fellow of the Royal Society, Edinburgh, who as Honorary Director, has brought the observations up to date.

The progress of Art, like education was also due to the direct encouragement of theRuler's of this state. The best samples of ancient sculpture in stone are to be seen in the principal temples of the country.

Some of them are so delicately and artistically chiselled that they deserve to be classed among real works of art. But it is doubtful if they can be called purely Travancorean. For we see everywhere the influence of the Dravidian style of architecture and sculpture. There can be no doubt that the workmen employed came from the other side of the ghauts. But in ivory carving Travancore has long attained a reputation which it still retains. We find that the Rajah who ascended the musnud in 1829 encouraged the art considerably,that during his time ivory workers from North Travancore brought "figures carved in ivory of so minute a size that they could be enclosed in a paddy husk" and that this was executed with implements no better than a country knife. The ivory-throne used by the Raja at Durbar was the best specimen of their skill.

Raja Marthanda Varma who succeeded him in 1846 evinced the same deep interest in the art and a state department was organised for the purpose. This was the beginning of the school of arts. Specimens of ivory works were sent to various exhibitions. In 1851 the Raja contributed to the International Exhibition (London) inaugurated by the late Prince Consort, an ivory throne. Her late Majesty the Queen Empress Victoria to whom it was presented wrote an autograph letter to the Raja commending its exquisite workmanship. The throne now adorns the state room in Windsor castle.

The presentation of the Royal autograph letter is the subject of an old painting by a European artist who visited the Maha Raja at that time. The picture is now in the Museum Library. It is an excellent memento of the event. Though the picture is not free from defects from the point of view of the present day artists, the figures are boldly drawn and are faithful reproductions of the principal personages represented.

The commencement of the progress of the art of painting may be said to date from the reign of Raja Rama Varma who has left an undying name by his musical compositions in Sanskrit, Malayalam and Telugu. He was a great patron of learning and his court was the rendezvous of great scholars and musicians. He invited men of talents from different parts of southern India and among these was Alagri Naidoo, a native of Madura, considered to be the best artist of the day. He was asked by the Raja to impart instruction in the art to Raja Raja Varma Koilthampuran of Kilimanoor who displayed in early life a remarkable taste in art. The pupil, as it not infrequently happens, excelled the master. He rose very high in the Raja's favour and soon came to be regarded as the greatest painter in Malabar. Although he possessed none of the facilities which the present day artists do, he became a past master of all the technicalities of the art and his drawings were extraordinarily faithful to nature and instinct with movement and life. Students from different parts of Travancore and Malabar poured fourth to sit at his feet and learn the art. He had about him a few of the most promising talents in the country in whom he evinced a fatherly interest. He loved the art for its own sake and soon became its devoted Votary all his life. What renders his devotion more remarkable is that when he became the head of the Killimanoor family, he voluntarily waived the right of management in favour of his cousin in order that he might follow his artistic inclinations and aptitudes unruffled by the cares of family-life.

To him, his nephew Ravi Varma Koil Tampuran is indebted for his renown as the greatest Indian Artist of the present day. He is the founder of a school of painting which has many followers and when the time comes, as it must come, for a history of painting to be written, his name will no doubt find the most prominent place in it. His works have awakened a general interest in the art throughout the length and breadth of India and his influence has created from end to end of the Empire an exquisite sense of the sublime and the beautiful. It is no exaggeration to say that in the life of Mr. Ravi

Varma is contained the history of the progress of painting specially in Travancore and generally in India.

Having received his early training from his talented uncle, he portrayed in eloquent colours scenes from the rich lore of the Hindu mythology. The visit of Mr. Theodore Jensen, an English portrait painter, to the court of Travancore was a turning point in the development of Ravi Varma's artistic capabilities. Mr. Ravi Varma who was a pet of the court on account of his extraordinary artistic skill, was introduced to the English artist who showed to him for the first time the immense possibilities that lay before him in the field of oil colours.

From this period Mr. Ravi Varma's real artistic career commenced. He painted first the portraits of the members of the Royal House in the new colours Despite the absence of scientific experts to guide him, despite the difficulty he has had to contend against in finding out a proper medium in which to grind his colours, without any systematic scientific training without any past records of experiments to rely on, Mr. Ravi Varma keeping Mr. Jensen's works before him as his models struck out a path for himself by his own genius and indometable industry. From concrete and real portraits he soared into the regions of imagination where his genius found full and free scope for building up his

MR. RAVI VARMA,

Koil Tampuran of Kilimanur.

reputation as an ideal painter. He won his first public recognition at the Fine Arts Exhibition of 1874 at which he won the Governor's medal for the picture of a Nair Lady at toilet of which the originality and naive beauty produced quite a sensation in the minds of the art-lovers of the southern satrapy.

His Highness the penultimate Maha Raja whose wise and prosperous reign obtained for the country the glorious appellation of a "Model state" took at once young Mr. Ravi under his patronage and assigned to him a studio in a part of his own palace. The first classical subject he painted was Sakuntala's love letter to Dushyanta which won him the Governor's gold medal in 1878. It had the privilege of being taken by His grace the Duke of Buckingham and Chandos whose portrait the artist painted later on for the Government house. His late Highness Vishakam Maha Raja who was an art critic as well, suggested to Mr. Ravi Varma, Seetha's ordeal as a subject which offered an ample scope for the exercise of the artist's talents. The picture found its way to the court of Baroda and, at the courteous invitation of the Gaekawar, the artist contributed a set of scenes from Indian mythology, some of which appear to have been sent to Europe. It is not our purpose to give an account of Ravi Varma's private life or to enumerate the names of princes and noblemen and statesmen who had sat to him for their portraits, but merely to show the amount of influence he has exercised on the rise and progress of the art in this country. He has done for art as no one has yet done in India. His greatness lies in having achieved the higher mission of art which in the words of Belzac "is not to copy nature but to express her, to seize the spirit, the soul and the expression of beings and things." He has brought to bear upon it whatever is pure and lofty. He has kindled the imagination with new conceptions and new beauties which have never before been the objects upon which the artist's pencil was employed. And since the subjects are drawn from the incidents vividly depicted in the Ramayana and the Mahabharata, every Hindu home is adorned with Ravi Varma's pictures and his name is remembered by his countrymen with an enthusiasm bordering on reverence. It is worthy of note that the talent for art runs in his family since his brother and only sister are also good painters as well. His brother Mr. Raja Raja Varma is his constant companion and coadjutor in the noble work. Unlike his brother, he is a realist and imbued with a strong spirit of modernism. It is as a landscape painter that he has won his laurels. He has won the highest rewards in art exhibitions for his treatment of landscape and *genre*. Some of his best works are exhibited in the Art Gallery now being formed under the auspices of the Fine Arts

Society in the Government Museum at Madras. The institution of an Art Gallery in our country under the presidentship of Mr. Ravi Varma owes its existence to the wisdom of the present Maharaja and the direct encouragement which it is his constant desire to bestow on the advancement of art. Mr. Ravi Varma has already contributed for a first instalment 3 puranic or quasi historic subjects in oil. The paintings are exhibited in the show room of the Industrial School of Arts. One is a representation of popular Sakuntala with her sylvan companions standing with one of her feet lifted and held up ostensibly to draw off a thorn from the sole of her foot but with the real purpose of catching a last glimpse of the form of her lover retreating from view. The second exhibits the royal court of King Virata where poor Draupadi fleeing from the lustful pursuit of wicked Kichaka is lying down flat before the august assemblage and in the very presence of her husbands in disguise, the sage pleading for justice, the cook thirsting for the blood of vengeance, but unable to do anything on account of their vow, Kichaka smitten with the pangs of lust chafing at the lost jewel and all the court beholding at outraged modesty and chastity. What a profound scene fit to move even the anger of a recluse.! The third is of Simhaka a deceitful wretch set up to mislead Draupadi in affright. These like his other productions are splendid illustrations of excellent poetic imagery, painted in colour, pointing to an exquisite sense of the sublime in nature and humanity. We cannot lay too much stress upon the usefulness of an art gallery as a state institution; on the policy that dictated it; on ths necessity of maintaining it on lives on which similar institutions such as the R. A.in London and elsewhere, are worked; on the advantages of inviting contributions from abroad and onthe immense possibility of the bright future that lay before the school of Arts along with the development of this branch of the institution.

CHAPTER VI.

RELIGIOUS AND CHARITABLE INSTITUTIONS.

The spirit of charity and sympathy is preeminently characteristic of the Hindus generally, and it forms, from time immemorial, the distinguishing attribute of the Maharajahs of Travancore. The noble devotion with which they enshrine Charity as the supreme divinity of their illustrious Royal House, has appropriately won for them the glorious appellation of Dharma Rajahs, and for their country that of Dharma Bhumi or the "land of charity." Having given the whole state as a free gift to Sri Padmanabha, the guardian God of the land, and made over the kingdom to the Devasvam, declaring that from that day (Fifth Medam, 925 Malabar Era) he was the vassal or agent of that deity and that he would conduct the affairs of the kingdom as a trustee of the Devasvam, the great Rama Varma assumed the title of Sri Padmanabha Dasa, which is retained to the present day. Whether this was superstition or policy, it is a fact nevertheless that as soon as peace was declared from one end of the country to the other the benevolence of the Maharajah showed itself in the large number of religious and charitable institutions throughout the country. Dewan Seshiah Sastri puts on record that there are fory-five such institutions throughout the state: that the chief one is at the capital, known as the Agrasala: that it is a very large institution of its kind and there is probably not the like of it in India, the arrangements for supplies, for custody and accounts of stores, and for cooking and serving being perfect and self-acting as it were: that the building forms an annexure of the great pagoda, in the extensive corridors and galleries of which the actual feeding daily takes place: and that the others are distributed at convenient stops on the line of the road commencing from the Aramboli pass in the south and ending at Parur in the north. Besides these Oottupuras, the large number of temples or pagodas also offer free fare Mr. Nagam Aiya notes :—"To about every big temple is attached an Oottupura in which an immense number of people, particularly, Brahmins, are daily fed."

These institutions are the outcome of religious and charitable endowments made by private individuals under the conviction that by doing so they would gain eternal beatitude. Both Brahmins and Nairs, (perhaps the latter more) have alike set apart extensive estates for the purpose from time out of mind. In view to add to these endowments and place them on a better footing likely to endure for all time to come, the benevolent tendency of the great Maharajahs to be the direct benefactors of the country and the people, led to the assumption of lands belonging to these institutions and the management of these institutions, under state control. It may be that the endowments were far in excess of the aggregate of actual expense and the State became a decided gainer by the bargain. But it goes without saying that it is a great trust that Government have solemnly undertaken to fulfil and are therefore bound to faithfully discharge to the very end. It will be useful to call some eminent witnesses who have expressed themselves in favour of the position advanced.

We will first call Mr. Shangunni Menon of the "Travancore History" fame. He says :— "Velu Tampi observing the various Devasvams in Travancore, the large estate each possessed, and the remarkable influence of the Devasvams over the people, contemplated the assumption of the whole and the annexation of the estate to the Sirkar, hoping by these means to neutralise, if not totally destroy the influence of the Devasvams over the people, and thus check any future commotions there might araise. On Colonel Munro being informed of this, he thought it important enough to be worthy of adoption. This measure was also the means of causing a permanent additional revenue to the State, for after meeting the expenses of the various Devasvams, it left a good margin in favour of the Sirkar."

We will next rely on the evidence of that model minister Seshiah Sastri. He says:—

"The Revenues of the lands belonging to this pagoda, which have been acquired from remote times by gifts, amount to Rs. 75,000 and go to defray the expenses of the institution, any surplus being credited to the State Treasury and any deficit, very rare, being made good from it." He continues:—"The State had no concern with the management of any temple before 987 Malabar Era, when the landed property of 378 temples was assumed by the State and the management taken over. The other minor temples 1171 in number which had no property were also assumed either before or after that date." He adds:—"The interest of Government in respect of these institutions, is, for the most part only that of trustee and even were it otherwise, this State will be bound as every other country in the world does, to maintain a church established out of public revenue." And lastly we will quote the opinion of the late Palace Sarvadhikaryakar Mr. Govinda Pillai. He points out that "In both classes of pagodas together (superior and inferior) the Government have charge of only 1295, while 8012 of them are the property of private bodies or ryots, that the private societies referred to as owning thousands of pagodas in the country are corporations of Namburi Brahmins or Pottis who from the surplus accumulation of their private property have contributed from time immemorial to the religious edification of their village communities." We can multiply authorities to show that the interest of Government in these institutions is that of a trustee. We trust these will suffice. The authorities adduced, show such a uniformity of opinion that any attempt to do away with these institutions is an attempt to break the solemn trust undertaken by Government.

At this distant of time it is impossible to trace these charities to their original authors. The difficulty is enhanced by the all absorbing charity of our Maharajas. The Brahmins came to enjoy free-feeding, for the popular conviction in those days was that the way to salvation varied directly with the number of Brahmins fed. Even to this day there are in the interior of the country which has not caught up the wave of the belligerent civilisation of the west, thousands of Hindus who cling obstinately and tenaciously to the same idea. We are sure this is a positive and practical proof of the utter baseness and baselessness of the idea that all this was worked up by interested priestcraft that was mostly benefited by it. We find everywhere lingering traces still of the Brahmins being a source of comfort and consolation to his non-Brahmin brethren in their temporal as well as spiritual welfare. We consider therefore that these institutions had their origin in pure piety and primitive simplicity. The management of these institutions was originally in the hands of the donors. After a time it fell into the hands of men whose piety to God was no more genuine than their temptation to defraud Him was powerful. It was at this stage that the Maharajas whose remarkable tendency is to be pre-eminently charitable, began to exercise a sort of personal supervision over these institutions. There is yet another and a stronger reason for this. In the struggle for supremacy between the Church and the State—a struggle that has arisen in all countries in the early stages of their development—the church triumphed here instead of the state as in Europe. Under the pressure of that triumph, the Maharajas were no less worshipful of the Brahmins than the people themselves. Impelled thus both by the spirit of the age as well as by their innate instinctive aptitude for charity, they gradually undertook the management in their own hands, solemnly assuring to carry out the terms of the endowments. It is a notorious fact that when the late Dewan, Mr. Ramiengar, assumed office, he attempted to divert the charity investments for the purpose of constructing Railways and other useful enterprises that might tap the resources of the country. He was told that these endowments were unprofitable; that they were mismanaged: that way-side Oottupuras, Chathrams, water-sheds and Mandapams established in days, when travelling was difficult and dangerous, were an anomaly in this age of progress and enlightenment when increased means of communication have made even the longest journey a source of ease and comfort; and that since the national genius of the race is able to find so many outlets for self preservation, the endowments of private charities might be put to better use. He too thought that in maintaining them he was countenancing a ridiculous waste. But when he came to know the sacred trust that Government have undertaken to fulfil, he at once held back and disdained to do any act that might tarnish the reputation of Government.

We shall next endeavour to ascertain the nature and classes of religious and charitable endowments. These come under two classes :— (1) those assumed and managed by Government; (2) those under private or mixed management. The latter admit of being classified into (1) endowments managed by corporate bodies; (2) endowments managed by private trustees; (3) endowments managed jointly by trustees and Government. Now as regards assumed endowments, it has been observed before that the State had no concern whatever with any temple prior to 984 M. E. More than one thousand and five hundred temples were assumed either at or after that date. The lands assumed now yield a revenue of over four lakhs of Rupees. Besides this there are other sources of income from the collections in the offering boxes and from Adiyara-fees of various kinds. The scale of expenditure is according to the importance of the temples. There are about a hundred temples in which it does not exceed a hundred rupees; there are over two hundred temples in which it does not go beyond one thousand rupees; there are seventy-five temples in which it varies from thousand rupees to six thousand rupees and there are seven other large and important temples, in four of which it rises to twelve thousand rupees and in the remaining three, the highest sum on record is thirty-two thousand rupees. The temple establishments contain four thousand hands in all, and it is well worth prominently remembering that of this, only about 1500 are Brahmins while all the rest belong to various other classes.

With regard to endowments managed by corporate bodies, Sir Seshia Sastri says:—"The most celebrated and venerated pagoda in the State, viz, that of Sri Padmanabhaswami, has a Government of its own unconnected with the State, the Sovereign having but half a vote among the governing body which consists of one Namburi Sannyasi, 16 Potti Brahmins and one Nair nobleman, (possessing with others a single vote) who constitute the honorary trustees."

We have already mentioned that the lands belonging to this pagoda were acquired by gifts and the annual revenue amounts to seventy-five thousand rupees. Towards its expenditure the State also contributes something. We find it recorded in one of the State administration reports—"it is on account of the two great Ootsavams, the two Bhadra-deepams or special ceremonies for the preservation of the crown and a few other ceremonies that occur periodically." We are sure no loyal subject of His Highness the Maharaja will question this item of expendi, rure, for in the words of the same authority "the State will be bound, as every other country in the world does, to maintain a church establishment out of Public Revenue." Under this head we should not omit to refer to the endowments whose management is vested in Samudayams or village corporations. We shall now proceed to speak of endowments managed by hereditary trustees. We find that in this class are included the institutions managed by the Sreepadom authorities; those managed by chieftains like the Edapallythampuran; and others under the control of Matams such as Athiyara, Kuvakara etc. The serpent kavoos attached to ancient houses are also of this description. To the same class belong special assignments for temple service such as lamp-lighting, incense-burning, garland-making, umbrella-holding, flag-bearing and the like. There is another species of the same kind of service known as Mandapappady. This obtains in the temples of South Travancore. It would appear that in the present settlement, the properties assigned for this kind of service are registered in the name of deities to whom they are dedicated and pattahs given to families performing the service. Of the classes of the temples contemplated in the last section, we would mention the Kosakode temple as an instance in point. It is quite analogous to the management of the Kaviyur temple before its management was taken over by Government.

It will be seen that the total number of temples assumed and managed by Government is a trifle when compared with their existing number. Mr,

Nagam Aiya puts down 83 per cent as outside Government management. He says; "The property owned by these 7,758 temples is also vast. According to the settlement of 1012 which comprised only a settlement of garden lands, these private Devasvams owned 54, 155 gardens, tax-free. The temples within the boundaries of Adhigara Olivu and Desa Olivu tracts are excluded from this calculation. The assessed rental of these 54, 155 gardens came to Rs. 79, 195. It can be safely estimated that the present assessment on them will come to 1½ lacs of Rupees. Multiplying this sum by 25, we get the figure 37 lacs of Rupees, the capitalized value of those gardens. The paddy lands of the same may be estimated to be worth about sixty lacs of Rupees in all. The landed properties of the Devasvams whose welfare it will be the object of this Bill to promote may be put down as worth one-crore of Rupees. The moveables of these temples may be valued at ⅓ of a crore, excluding the buildings almost all of which are in different stages of decay throughout the country. These are the properties known to the public accounts before 1012. Properties purchased since then in the name of those temples or properties dedicated to them or to other charities before that date, if paying Sirkar tax cannot be discovered from the Sirkar accounts. These also will swell the property of the institutions. It may not be far wrong if I estimate that the total value of the endowments meant to be dealt with is about 2 crores of Rupees." We can without any fear of contradictiou aver that the picture of capitalized wealth presented by Mr. Nagam Aiya is by no means an overdrawn one. Regarding the data furnished by him, the late Mr. Chellappa Pillai justly observes, "Mr. Nagam Aiya has, at great pains, done what a Royal Commission in England did in 36 years at a cost of two hundred and forty thousand pounds." Too much stress cannot be laid on the necessity of the preservation of charitable institutions.

We find that at all times, in all societies, and under all systems of Government the poor element has been a great source of trouble and annoyance to the State. At present this is the one insoluble problem in Western societies. Imperial Rome was able to maintain peace in her metropolis only by catering to the needs and freaks of her poor citizens, and Consuls and Tribunes saved their honor and life at the sacrifice of their wealth. In England, society was thrown in a ferment and the poor laws were passed. A huge mass of starving poverty acted as a ready cumbustible heap to catch the sparks of revolution and largely contributed to perpetrate all those dark atrocities of the French Revolution. The most difficult question in practical politics now is to make the clamouring of the poor innocuous and to prevent the centralization of wealth. Happily, the Travancore Maharajahs are free from all these difficulties, and we are strongly disposed to attribute this happy state of affairs to the extensive charities, both aided and private, that are being carried on from one end of the land to the other.

Conclusion. During the period under notice, Travancore had the singular good fortune of having on its throne a succession of very enlightened Maha Rajahs. The commencement of progress on modern lines is contemporaneous with the assumption of direct Government of India by Her late illustrious Majesty Victoria the Good, and the first Imperial assemblage at Delhi for declaration of the same. The auspicious occasion of the second Imperial assemblage in connection with the Coronation of Her son and successor, our King-Emperor Edward VII, affords now a fitting opportunity of taking stock o the progress the country has made. It will be seen that the beneficent influence of the paramount power has been increasingly brought to bear upon the administration of affairs. His Highness the present Maha Rajah has gratefully acknowledged: "My house has been fortunate enough to ally itself to the great British power in India from the earliest times, and to that alliance I owe the Musnud on which I sit, for it saved the country at a critical time and has maintained it in peace ever since. To the influence of Her Majesty's supremacy is due also whatever of prosperity and enlightenment Travancore has attained to, for her representatives have guided our footsteps in the path of progress and her country. men have contributed largely to raise our people and develop our resources." It was therefore no idle sentiment that Lord Ampthill expressed when he claimed the fact that the Madras Government had largely contributed to the successful and enlightened administration of the state by freely giving to Travancore in the past some of British India's best intellect and great ability in the persons of Sir Madava Row and Sir Seshia Sastri and we may also add Dewan Ramaiengar. These belong to a brilliant galaxy of Indian statesmen who have acquired for themselves a name in history. The service rendered by Sir Madava Row cannot be exaggerated. He not only rescued the country from political extinction but acquired for it the proud appellation of a "Model State." His erudite Highness the late Maha Raja thought "what Pericles did for Athens, what Cromwell did for England, that Sir Madava Row did for Travancore". Sir Seshia Sastri and Dewan Ramaiengar have by their administrative ability compelled the admiration of the British Government. It was during their time that the wave of modern progress caught up Travancore in its course and extended its fertilising conquest over the country. Since the accession of the present Maha Rajah, the Diwanate was successively filled by the energies and intelligence of officers from the local service. Mr. Rama Row, a kinsman of the illustrious Sir Madava Row, was the first to hold the office. In appreciation of his service, His Highness the Maha Rajah feelingly wrote to him thus on the eve of his retirement:—

"Thoroughly loyal to your sovereign, true to the best interests of the state, and deeply interested in the welfare of my subjects, you have done all that could be done to secure those interests and advance that welfare to the best of your means and power." Dewan Shungarasoobyer, a true son of the soil, succeeded him. That he earned that position by his character and his talents is approved and applauded by the Government of Madras who considered that his administration was "vigorous and efficient" and that the Travancore state "owes a debt of gratitude for his long and meritorious service." The success of his successor Dewan Behauder Krishnaswamy Row, a finished product of the British Indian judicial system, whose service as its Chief Justice Travancore owed to the generosity of the Madras Government, was foretold by no less a person than Sir P. P. Hutchins, a member of the council of the Secretary of State for India, who wrote that he "has thoroughly established his ability as an administrator and proved the principle that good judges generally make good administrators." This is in harmony with the "marvellous progress and a very high

DEWAN BAHADUR K. KRISHNASWAMI RAO, C.I.E.

standard of administration" reported by the Resident to the Government of Madras.

For our part, we hold it is always manly, like the proverbial swan that drinks only the milk and leaves the water behind, to acknowledge the good a man has done. We consider that these have done nobly by Travancore and their Diwanates are marked by the initiation of several measures of reform; measures for improving and expanding the revenue of the state; measures for the promotion of trade and commerce, by providing facilities for internal and external communication and the removal of existing disabilities; measures for the improvement of municipal and other public institutions; measures for a system of general and technical education; measures for the revival of drooping industries and the development of the resources of the country. None can rejoice more than the people over the responsibility the Maha Rajah has undertaken when he solemnly avowed to them: "To promote your welfare will be my highest aim; to witness your prosperity and happiness, my best reward." Lord Ampthill only sustains the vast burden of that responsibility by the assurance that "it is one of the most interesting concerns of the Madras Government to be in close political alliance with Travancore and that those relations are wholly smooth and pleasant is a natural consequence of that loyal attachment of the rulers of Travancore to the British Crown and of the admirable administration which has won for Travancore the designation of a "Model State."